T0245749

JUDGES

OTHER
BIBLICAL CHARACTER STUDIES
BY WALTER C. KAISER, JR.

The Lives and Ministries of ELIJAH and ELISHA

ABRAHAM The Friend of God

JOSHUA A True Servant Leader

The Journey from JACOB to ISRAEL

JOSEPH From Prison to Palace

NEHEMIAH The Wall Builder

THE TWELVE The "Minor" Prophets Speak Today

ZECHARIAH The Quintessence of Old Testament Prophecy

SAMUEL The SEER First In The Prophetic Movement In Israel

DANIEL The Man Highly Esteemed By God

JUDGES When Times of Peace or Judgment Reigned

RUTH & ESTHER Women of the Providence of God

— —

COMING SOON

EZEKIEL Study of Israel In The Last Days

DAVID A Man After God's Own Heart

MOSES The Man Who Saw the Invisible God

SOLOMON The King with a Listening Heart

JUDGES

When Times of Peace
and Judgment Reigned

Walter C. Kaiser, Jr.

Lederer Books
An imprint of
Messianic Jewish Publishers
Clarksville, MD 21029

© 2024 Walter C. Kaiser, Jr. All rights reserved.

No part of this publication may be reproduced, stored in a retrieval system, or transmitted in any form or by any means without the prior permission of the publisher, except for brief reviews in magazines, or as quotations in another work when full attribution is given.

Unless otherwise noted, all Scripture quotations are taken from the New American Standard Bible. Nashville: Thomas Nelson Publishers, 1978; the Complete Jewish Bible, Baltimore: Messianic Jewish Publishers, 1998; or the New International Version Bible, New York: International Bible Society, 2002.

Cover design by Lisa Rubin, Messianic Jewish Publishers
Graphic Design by Yvonne Vermillion, MagicGraphix.com
Editing by George August Koch

Cover art by Gustave Doré, an Alsacian artist, most famous for his depictions of numerous scenes from the Bible.

ISBN: 978-1-951833-37-4

Printed in the United States of America

Published by:
Lederer Books
An imprint of Messianic Jewish Publishers
6120 Day Long Lane
Clarksville, MD 21029

Distributed by:
Messianic Jewish Publishers & Resources
Order line: (800) 410-7367
lederer@messianicjewish.net
www.MessianicJewish.net

Table of Contents

Lesson 1

A Theological Evaluation
of the Conquest of Canaan
Judges 2:1–3:5

The second chapter of the book of Judges opens with an account of a second great assembly of God's people Israel in session. Previously the tribes had met with great fear and anxiety about facing the Canaanites as they asked the Lord which tribe should lead the attack against the Canaanites. He had answered that it was the tribe of Judah.

On this occasion, however, the nation of Israel was told by "the Angel of the LORD" of "their unfaithfulness," and that God would no longer drive out the Canaanites and go up into battle before Israel, because of their disobedience to his commands and teaching. This word from the Lord turned the occasion into a time of deep mourning and weeping. Hence the name given to that place was Bokim, meaning "Weepers."

The word "Canaanite" denoted the culture more precisely rather than a particular ethnic group. In general, however, this term covered mainly a Semitic population living in the second millennium B.C.E. that inhabited Syria and the land of Canaan that God had promised to Israel.[1]

"Bokim" was likely named in remembrance of the outpouring of their grief, sorrow and weeping before the Lord, when they were told by the angel that God, would no longer drive out the enemy from the land the people of Israel were attempting to inhabit. Who was this "angel of the LORD," who had come up from the village of Gilgal at Bokim? Some conjecture that he was the High Priest for that year; others think he was a prophet commissioned to bring a particular message to the people. But he

---

1. J. Gray, *The Canaanites*, in Arthur E. Cundell, *Judges* (1968), 64–65.

was neither a priest nor a mortal prophet, though the Hebrew word translated "angel" can also be rendered "messenger."

Instead, he is best seen as the second person of the Trinity, the very same one the Lord had promised he would send before Israel as the "Captain of the LORD's host" (Josh. 5:14), the same One who carried Israel all the days of old (Isa. 63:9). This "messenger," or "envoy," of the Lord occurs 19 times in Judges and thrice as the "Messenger of Elohim." But in these cases, the "messenger" is a heavenly person, since in Judges 6:8 and 11:1 there is a clear distinction between the prophet and the one sent from heaven. He was no doubt the same individual the Lord promised in Exodus 23:20–23, who had been sent ahead of Israel in the time of Moses, and the one who had announced himself as "the Captain of the LORD's host." Likewise, when Manoah and his wife saw the "angel of the LORD," it was the same thing as seeing God himself (Judg. 13:22).

The evidence of the Lord's presence in the midst of the people was linked with the tabernacle, which was carried with them as they journeyed through the desert. When Israel crossed the Jordan River, the tabernacle was set up in Gilgal, then moved to Bokim, whose location is unknown. However, the Septuagint reads that it was sent to "Bokim and to Bethel and to the house of Israel." This suggests Bokim was the same place also called Bethel, for elsewhere in the text, the sanctuary is located at Bethel (Judg. 20:18–28; 21:1–4). Others support this possible link by noting that the two names can be found linked together in Genesis 35:8, where Rebekah's nurse, Deborah, was buried beneath "the oak of weeping" near Bethel. Later the tabernacle was moved in Joshua's day to the site of Shiloh, where it remained for most of the campaigns under Joshua (Josh. 98:6; 10:6–9, 15, 43; 14:6). So, let us examine this text of Scripture.

We Too Fail to Respond to the Lord's Chastisements – 2:1–5

Against the backdrop of the Lord's gracious actions on behalf of Israel in the past, God records his displeasure with his people in their more recent responses to his work on their behalf. He pointed to those past actions of his that should be recalled to the minds of the people of Israel. God had brought them up out of Egypt (2:1); he had led them into the land he had sworn he would give them (2:1b); and he had told them he would never break his covenant with them (2:1c). Indeed, his angel had led Israel just as he had promised to do so long ago (Exod. 23:20–23).

In light of all he had done for them, Israel was not to make any covenants (Hebrew *berit*, "alliances, agreements") with the people of the land (2:2a). No doubt the writer had in mind the unwise agreement Joshua made with the Gibeonites (Josh. 9:1–26), or the covenantal kindness (*hesed*) the Ephraimites made with the man from Bethel (Judg. 1:29). Instead, God's people were to break down the altars of the pagan gods (2:2). This language recalls the injunctions found in Deuteronomy 7:1–5 and 12:1–3, as well as Exodus 34:13.

The Lord accused the nation of Israel of transgressing his covenant with them (2:2b). He asked, "Why have you done this?" (2:2c). He affirmed that he would no longer drive out Israel's enemy ahead of them; instead, the enemy would become "thorns in their sides" and their gods would become "a snare to them" (2:3). After the angel had spoken these things, the Israelites "wept aloud" and named the place "Bokim," even as they attempted to offer sacrifices to the Lord. However, such sacrifices could hardly have been sincere, for they were merely done by rote and not by any sort of genuine repentance or by an authentic demonstration of godly sorrow (2:4). God wanted from the people the precise things he would later again speak of in Joel 2:12–13—

> "Return to me with all your heart, with fasting and weeping and mourning…. Tear open your heart and not your garments."

Another reminder of what God wanted could be found by them in the teaching given in 1 Samuel 15:22b…

> To obey is better than sacrifice and to harken than the fat of rams.

It was clear that God's presence and power were what made the difference for those who were caught in a time of national crisis. Success in life, and even gains on the battlefield, came not from the east or the west, nor from the superiority in the quality of the weapons used; that success was always a result of the powerful intervention on a people's behalf by God himself.

If mortals would not honor and obey the Lord and his commands and promises, then the flip side of obedience was the devastation God would bring for disobedience in his judgments and the triumphs of the enemy over the people of God. It is very foolish to disobey the Lord and to follow after and worship pagan gods; it will provoke his sure judgment!

We Too Often Forget Those Who Have Led Us – 2:6–9

Judges 2:6 seems to be a summary of Joshua 24:29–31. It also appears that under Joshua's leadership, he had broken the back of the Canaanite resistance in the land of Canaan. However, there still was a great deal more to be conquered on a local level. So, after a covenant renewal ceremony, which may have taken place at Shechem or Mount Ebal, Joshua dismissed the tribes to complete the task of occupying the land. Therefore, the Israelites now had a second chance to finish and to clean up the job that had been begun under Joshua. It also was true that the Israelites remained faithful and loyal to the Lord all the days of Joshua and as long as the elders who had been with him during his lifetime were still alive.

But how long did this period of faithfulness under Joshua's influence last? We are not told how long Joshua lived after the events of Judges 2:1–5. But it's reasonable to guess that Joshua was in his 80s year when Israel crossed the Jordan ca. 1405 B.C.E. Based on Joshua 14:7, 10, it appears the initial conquest of the land took about seven years. When Joshua died at the age of 110, he had served an additional 10–20 years after breaking the back of the Canaanite opposition, so we are around 1390 B.C.E.

If the leaders at the head of the nation of Israel continued their commitment to the Lord, then the people tended to follow them and the conditions in the Covenants God had made with Abraham, Isaac and Jacob. The people held Joshua and the elders in high esteem as their examples of godly living. Together with these leaders, the people had seen the mighty works God had done for Israel. Some of the children may have seen the parting of the Red Sea, but now, in this new generation, all of them had seen the waters of the Jordan part. They had witnessed the collapse of Jericho and seen five southern Canaanite kings all captured at one time in a cave where they had gone to hide. They knew God was rich in his grace toward them as the people of God, but how quickly after the time of Joshua and the days of the elders the people forgot all that God had done on their behalf.

Joshua died and was buried in the land of his inheritance at Timnath Heres, in the hill country of Ephraim (2:9), which in Joshua 24:30 is called "Timnath-serah." If that is an accurate reading of the text, then by transposing the letters of the second word it becomes "Heres," signifying the "sun." Could it be that the Jewish memory of this site was one that was marked as a memorial of the day Israel elected to honor God for the time when the sun stood still at Joshua's command, while Israel completed the battle they had begun at Gibeon (Josh. 10:1–14)?

We Too Forget God and What He Has Done For Us – 2:10–15

Once Joshua's generation was gathered to the Lord after his death, another generation arose after them who "did not know the LORD" (2:10). That was the same phrase that was used to describe the two priestly sons of Eli; they "did not know [or 'had no regard for'] God" (1 Sam. 2:12). These Israelites had no practical or real deep experience with the Lord who had been so good to their forefathers and delivered the land to them. Instead of serving the Lord, this new generation did evil in God's sight and deliberately served the false gods known as Baals, such as Baal Peor, Baal-Zebub, or Baal-Zephan.

Israel's loss of any historical memory of her past led to her apostasy. Herein lies a warning to the believing body in all ages: When we let slip the memory of the tremendous ways in which our Lord has come to our aid time after time, and we care little or nothing for all God's mercies, we are well on the way to apostasy. When we deny the One who bought us by his blood on the cross, we are in need of being rescued from our sins.

Moreover, it will become evident that when we go to face our enemies in battle, "the hand of the LORD [will then be] against us" (2:15). Our Lord had warned us that this would be the result of our departing from him and his word and our forgetting all that he had done for us.

There is a real difference between knowing about God and our personally experiencing him in real worship of his person and work.

Ignorance and plain forgetfulness of all that God has done in the past for our forefathers, and for us in the meantime, is inexcusable. The prophet Malachi taught that there was a difference between those who feared the LORD and who "thought on" or "meditated on" him and reflected on his name versus those who never saw such a distinction (Mal. 3:16). Too often today some church attenders say they know who God is, but they care little or nothing for his name or reputation, much less give any thought to all his works on their behalf.

We Too Forget God Delivered Us by His Leaders – 2:16–23

In the midst of the rehearsal of all of Israel's sin, there comes a surprising note of grace from God in v. 16. God raised up "judges" who would "save" Israel. How or why the Lord called these men and women "judges" is not detailed here, for it may have been by a secret prompting of a man's spirit, in view of the awful calamities and sufferings the people were facing, that this name was selected. However, this inward movement of the man's spirit was typically followed by an express call of a divine command from on high to accept the work of leading a hurting people. Usually, these same individuals displayed some act of heroism, or some miraculous exploitation, as can be especially illustrated in the lives of Gideon and Samson. Nevertheless, God raised these judges up to save Israel from the hands of these raiders and conquerors.

The Israelites, though, responded to God's loving action in an ungrateful and treacherous way (2:17). Israel still went on a rampage of chasing after Baals and other false gods as they yielded to the whims of the surrounding culture. In fact, Judges describes seven times over the seven apostasies of the Israelites (2:11; 3:7; 3:12; 4:1; 6:1; 10:6; 13:1). The Canaanite god Baal, as he appeared in native mythology, was the son of the senior god El, and was designated as the god of storm and fertility. The worship of Baal remained one of the key distractions for Israel all the way up to the Babylonian captivity in 586 B.C.E., when Jerusalem and the temple were decimated by the conqueror Nebuchadnezzar in 586 B.C.E.

Baal's consort was Ashtaroth (or Ashtoreth), the mother goddess of love, war and fertility. Her name and worship in ancient Sumer was Inaana, but in Babylon she was Ishtar, and in northern Syria she was called Anat.

God chastened Israel by delivered them into the hands of their enemies (Deut. 32:21–22). The nations, whose false gods the Israelites worshiped, became the nations that ruled over Israel time after time (Lev. 26:37), not to mention the obvious fact that the "hand of the LORD was against [the people of Israel]" (Lev. 26:17; Deut. 28:25, 41–42). When Israel went hard after these pagan gods, the nation of Israel that had been virtually married to God thereby exhibited in each and every case a violent breach of that covenant that they were involved in spiritual prostitution and adultery. No wonder, then, that God needed to raise up judges to save his people. But what's amazing is that the narrative begins immediately without any evidence of a revival on the part of the people! In fact, this is typical of Judges: The Lord intervenes on Israel's behalf in a pure act of mercy and solely on the basis of divine compassion and grace (2:16).

Verse 18 not only tells us that God raise up judges, but it also affirms that he was with them as well as he delivered Israel from the hands of their oppressors because the plight and "groanings" of the people caused the Lord to "repent" (2:18b). The Hebrew word rendered "repent," *naham*, actually means "to regret, to relent, to grieve" (cf. Gen. 6:6–7; Deut. 32:36). Despite the merciful treatment given to Israel by God, when the judge was dead, guess what happened repeatedly (2:19)? The people of Israel "returned" to their pagan former ways. In fact, now they went even further into the more corrosive effects of sin than their fathers had gone before them (2:19b). They persisted in following after other gods besides the LORD God who had delivered them, thus Israel refused to cease from going on their stubborn and persistent paths of sin (2:19c).

Israel forgot the covenant they had made with God, which caused his anger to burn hot against them (2:20). They refused to listen to his voice (2:20c). So the rest of this chapter basically repeats the substance of what the angel of the Lord told them earlier. No longer would God "drive out" from Israel the nations that opposed them (2:21). He would allow those nations to continue to harass Israel "to prove" them as to "whether they would keep the way of the LORD, as their fathers did, or not" (2:21c). Consequently, the Lord left those nations as conquering rulers of Israel—without driving them out of Israel hastily. That is why Joshua did not finish driving out these hostile nations. The reason is the same as the one given in v. 22.

We Too Forgot That God Can Even Use Adversity in Our Lives – 3:1–5

The Lord had purposely left certain nations in the land of Canaan to assess and to prove Israel. First to be mentioned were the five lords of the Philistine pentapolis living in the Gaza Strip (3:3a), for few nations gave Israel more trouble in their history than the Philistines. They were not native to Canaan, but they were part of the Sea Peoples who came into Canaan from Anatolia (modern Turkey) and the Mediterranean area late in the 12th century B.C.E. The Bible identifies Crete (or Caphtor) as their place of origin (Gen. 10:13–14; Amos 9:7; Jer. 47:4). An earlier wave of these people may have used the southwestern coastal area of the Gaza Strip as a prior source for raising food for the Philistines, who at the time were living perhaps on the island of Crete, before they made their permanent move to reside in this area in Canaan. Their cities in Canaan included Ashkelon, Ashdod, Ekron, Gath and Gaza.

Among the other nations God used to prove his people Israel were "all the Canaanites," which no doubt referred to the inhabitants of Canaan in general (3:3). Next mentioned were the Sidonians, which often referred to all the Phoenicians (see Gen. 10:15, where Sidon is called the "son of Canaan"). Another group of opponents to Israel were the Hivites, who generally lived in the area north of the Sea of Galilee in the Lebanon mountains and possibly at the foot of Mount Hermon. Thus, this list tended to represent the entire land of Canaan—the area in the southwest (occupied by the the Philistines), the northwest (occupied by the Sidonians), the northeast (occupied by the Hivities) and the southeast (where the Canaanites were). The failure of Israel to obey the Lord represented the entire area of Canaan occupied by all the tribes of Israel.

In addition to the Lord's deliberate didactic decision not to clear the whole land of the pagan inhabitants of Canaan, there also was a probationary purpose, as seen in Judges 3:4. This can be seen in the two infinitives in v. 4: "To test Israel through [these nations]" and "to determine" whether they would or would not express allegiance to God by the way they heeded the Torah of Moses.

There is, as it were, a report card on how Israel fared in the test and the evidential testimony of Israel with regard to these two areas in which God was watching over them to see how they would fare. The verdict was not good, for Israel failed in her performance in three particularly important areas (3:5–6). First, the descendants of Israel settled down in the midst of the Canaanites, Hittites, Amorites, Perizzites, Hivites and Jebusites (3:5). Of the seven Canaanite nations listed in Deuteronomy 7:1, only the name of the Girgashites is missing now from the earlier list. God had warned them not to settle with these pagan nations, but that is what she did!

But Israel also failed in another area, for they intermarried with the Canaanites, in direct violation of Deuteronomy 7:3–4. Examples of this type of failure can be seen in judge Gideon, who married a Shechemite concubine to produce a son "Abimelech" (Judg. 8:29ff), while Gilead's marriage to a prostitute produced "Jephthah" (Judg. 11:1) and Samson's marriage to a Philistine woman that also ended tragically (Judg. 14–16).

The third failure of Israel could be seen in her violation of the first principle of the covenant as the nation served other gods. Israel was to have no other gods beside the Lord, but that is what she indulged in more and more. The theme of the book of Judges is struck early in this book. Israel's territorial accommodation easily resulted in her Canaanization of her spiritual situation and ethical practices. What is most surprising, however, is that the Lord would continue to intervene on their behalf as a nation!

Conclusions

1. Judges 2:1 began with the Lord affirming "[he would] never break [his] covenant with Israel." This is amazing loving-kindness given Israel's response!

2. Israel was warned from the beginning not to make a covenant with the people of the land of Canaan, nor to dwell with them or live alongside them in the land of Canaan.

3. The "angel of the LORD" announced at the beginning of Judges emphasized that if the nation failed to obey, the Lord would no longer drive these foreigners out of the land. This sad note sent the nation into a major season of weeping and mourning.

4. Israel aroused the anger of God by forsaking him and doing evil in his eyes. They served and worshiped the gods of these nations, so the Lord delivered them into the hands of their enemies.

5. The Lord left Israel living in the midst of six hostile nations in order to test her and to determine if she would fully follow him in all her ways.

Lesson 2

Judge Othniel and the Aram-Naharaim Oppression

Judges 3:7–11

Judges 3:7 begins the second major section of this book; it goes to 16:31 and covers seven oppressors Israel endured including the seven judges God raised up to meet their attack on his people. In fact, the refrain will become somewhat boring. The narrative begins with "The Israelites did evil in the eyes of the LORD, then they forgot the LORD their God, and thus they tragically ended up serving other Baals and Asherahs" (3:7). Thus, Israel was guilty of two sins: They deliberately "forgot" the Lord, who was their own God, and they "served" the false gods Asherah and Baal.

Othniel was the man who received Caleb's daughter Achsah as his wife as a reward for his overthrowing and conquering the town of Kiriath-Sepher, meaning "town of the book/scroll" (a.k.a. Debir; Josh. 15:15, 19; Judg. 1:11–15). He was the son of Kenaz, Caleb's younger brother (Josh. 15:15–16; Judg. 1:13) who had shown his abilities by conquering Kiriath-Sepher. This not only signaled his valor and his leadership abilities, but it gave him a reputation that showed he was particularly qualified to lead his people in a war to gain their freedom from this Mesopotamian attacker!

Othniel was the only judge to come from the southern tribes. His task was to face the Mesopotamian king Cushan-Rishathaim (Judg. 3:7–11), meaning "Cushan the doubly wicked." This was no doubt a nickname, but it also served as a mocking pseudonym given to him by the Israelites.

The Spirit of the LORD Came Upon Him

The expression "The Spirit of the LORD came upon him" is extremely important in our understanding of God's role in calling "judges" or "deliverers" in this book. This expression is found in four other places in this book (6:34; 11:29; 14:19; 15:14). There are an additional three places where the same expression is used in 1 Samuel (11:6; 16:13–14).

Unfortunately, the view persists among many believers that the Holy Spirit (*Ruach HaKodesh*) operated differently in the Old Testament than in the New Testament. The traditional view is to say that the Spirit of God just "came upon" Old Testament believers episodically and momentarily, while in the New Testament the Spirit constantly dwelt in the believers, i.e., they were permanently "indwelt."[1] This view ignores the continuity of the Holy Spirit's operations in the older testament, so it doesn't interpret this expression satisfactorily. There is a more physical and metaphorical equivalent expression: "the hand of the LORD came upon [so-and-so]," which has a more urgent claim and a sense of overwhelming force with which God operates. Thus, as the third member of the Holy Trinity, the "Spirit of God" comes on individuals, showing his arresting power and presence so that those who might otherwise be unqualified or indisposed to serve the Lord are divinely equipped. Thus it seems best not to deny the "indwelling of the Holy Spirit's work" in the Old Testament.

Moreover, it is difficult to suggest an Old Testament person could be regenerated without the Holy Spirit indwelling the believer. The verse most believers use to counter this teaching is John 14:17, which says the Spirit "abides/resides with you and *will be* [or: '*is*'] in you." But even this verse, that some claim teaches that the indwelling will occur at some future event, clearly teaches the Spirit is already "abiding" or "residing" in the believer. Further, there is good Hebrew manuscript evidence to read instead that the Holy Spirit already "*is*" in believers! And in John 7:37–39, on the Feast of Tabernacles, where traditionally there was the water-pouring ceremony (cf. Zech. 14:8, 16–18), Yeshua taught on this occasion that the believer would experience "from within him" a pouring forth of "streams of living water."

---

1. See Richard Averbeck's excellent article "The Holy Spirit in the Hebrew Bible and Its Connections with the New Testament" in *Who's Afraid of the Holy Spirit? An Investigation Into the Ministry of the Spirit of God Today*, ed. M. James Sawyer and Daniel Wallace (2005), especially 30-36.

Likewise, Yeshua's encounter with the woman at the well in John 4:10, 14 did not mean the Holy Spirit did not yet exist, but that here was another experience that was much like that of Nicodemus' learning session with Yeshua when he rebuked Rabbi Nicodemus for not knowing these things about the Spirit despite being a teacher of the Jewish people. Acts 19:2 is another case where the disciples of Ephesus were functioning much as Nicodemus was, for they too were ignorant about indwelling of the Spirit.

To be sure, there is a difference between the testaments, but it was not that one testament had the Holy Spirit constantly indwelling in the believer and the other did not. Instead, the difference was that the Holy Spirit was not yet active in the lives of believers in the way he would be after Yeshua was glorified (i.e., the Lord would baptize them all into one corporate body), but God's Holy Spirit was actively indwelling believers in both testaments.

Let's look at this section that treats Othniel's judgeship more distinctly.

When We Do Evil in the Eyes of the LORD – 3:7

The writer opened his series of Israel's oppressors and her deliverers with the simplest and most paradigmatic case of all. The account of Othniel's deliverance of Israel from the Mesopotamian incursion into the land is so skeletal and gives so a minimal details that it functions well as a paradigm or a model for those other six judges and deliverances that follow. It also serves well as an example and an outline of how progressive and persistent was the moral and spiritual degeneration that followed. We are not told which of the tribes were involved in this apostasy of the people of Israel, nor exactly where this mysterious Cushan-Rishathaim came from, nor what preparation, if any, was given to Othniel to carry out this task. And we wonder just how he won the victory over this Mesopotamian monarch. The details are indeed slim, but it is clear that some or all of Israel had gone apostate as they lived and settled down among the six foreign nations that Israel had been told to "drive out of the land." Added to all this, they had married the daughters of these nationalities and had promptly forgotten the Lord and served their gods.

The evil Israel engaged in was unquestionably awful. The standard of right and wrong was one measured by the character and word of God; therefore there could be no debate over whether or not Israel had sinned against God! The most pronounced act of evil, however, was the nations' abandonment of the God who loved them and had called them. This led to a loss of memory of who God was and all he had done for Israel in the previous years. This was then followed by the substitution of worshiping a host of other gods in place of the worship of the Living God.

All such evil was done in the eyes of the Lord. He was both the inspector of evil and the standard for what was good and what was to be preferred by his people. Such service of the pagan gods, who were just zeroes and downright "nothings," brought about a real captivity and the bondage of Israel, for only service to the Living God could set any of them free.

When God Gives Us Over to an Oppressor – 3:8

For the next 8 years, Israel was held captive by this king Cushan from somewhere in Mesopotamia. This all happened as a result of the strong wrath of God against sin. His judgment, however, was also simultaneously a sign of hope, but unfortunately for this degenerate people, they were too bound by sin to recognize it. Thus, Cushan-Rishathaim, nicknamed "Cushan of double wickedness," is left to pull his treachery on Israel, just as the prophet Jeremiah later named the city and people of Babylon "Merathaim," which too means "double wickedness," because of the treachery they would later work against Israel. This in spite of the Lord's clear calling out and declaring what was evil in both cases. Had he not cared about the people he had sent judgment to, he would not have singled out this evil, for despite judgment, he showed that he still cared for them. To speed up the recovery of his people, the Lord "sold" his people into the power of Cushan. Then they cried out to the Lord.

When We Cry Out to the Lord for Help – 3:9

Israel's response to this eight years of servitude to Cushan-Rishathaim was finally to cry out mightily to the Lord. But this did not seem a penitential plea of repentance; it was a cry of distress and pain, a call for help and relief. It was a cry that comes in times of distress as first seen in Exodus 2:23.

But if this was not a cry of repentance on the part of the people, then why did God respond? It was because he saw the misery of the people he continued to love as he had called for them to be his avenue for blessing the whole world. This illustrates God's way of moving in history. When God's people are unfaithful, he gives his people into the hand of an oppressor. However, when that oppressor gets too big for his own good and deludes himself into acting and believing that he is lord instead of recognizing the Living God as sovereign over all, then God brings down that leader. In Jeremiah 27:5–7, Jeremiah taught that God hands nations over to whomsoever it seems right to do so, but there is a time when that kingdom he uses to punish his people must be brought down, for that nation's arrogance, and oppression of other nations as well, is offensive to our Lord and it too must be corrected by God's judgment. Jeremiah states that is to be "until the time of his own land comes" (Jer. 27:7, RSV). The Lord God is the Lord of history, for both our times and history's times—both are in the hands of the Lord, for he alone is the One who grants deliverance.

When God Grants Us Deliverance – 3:10–11

The Spirit of God came upon Othniel, and in this manner he became a judge over Israel. Perhaps he was moved or acted upon by supernatural influence to take the lead in delivering his people from being under the reign of Cushan. In this case, Othniel was no doubt endowed with valor, strength, and fortitude to do the work he was called to. In this role he not only administered the role of intervening in the work of resolving local disputes, but he was at the head of the forces facing the enemy and ridding them of their eight years of oppression and distress.

It is said that the land enjoyed 40 years of quietude and rest after God gave deliverance from eight years of Cushan's oppression. These 40 years must have been calculated from the time Othniel began his rule to deliver Israel. It also seems the length of the years of rest lasted up until the time Othniel died. This shows how important and how powerful the presence of one good man is to the life of a nation, a congregation or a people.

Conclusions

1. The study of this judge contains by and large only the bare essentials of apostasy, the oppression by an oppressor, and the outcry of the people to the Lord, which ended in their deliverance. This set of essentials give us a paradigmatic case for the rest of the narratives about the judges.

2. The same Lord who sold Israel into the hands of the oppressor is the same Lord who delivers her out of her sin and misery.

3. 1 Timothy 2:2 teaches us to pray for "kings and all those in authority, that we may live peaceful and quiet lives in all godliness and holiness."

4. So, few details are given about Othniel that there is nothing of a flashy or spectacular aura about him.

Lesson 3

Judge Ehud Stops the Oppressor, King Eglon of Moab
Judges 3:12–30

Already the phrase "the Israelites did evil in the eyes of the LORD" is growing almost tiresome even though the book of Judges is just beginning. While God's indictment of Israel's sin could be described in greater elaborate detail, what we read here of her spiritual problem is enough to indicate that the nation is in for trouble once again as it has abandoned God!

God's new response to Israel's penchant for sinning was to give "Eglon king of Moab power over Israel" (3:12b). This subjugation to the nation of Moab was most remarkable, for not only were the Moabites not among the list of nations God had left in the land to test Israel (3:3–6), but they were descendants from Abraham's nephew Lot (Gen. 19:36–37). Moreover, the fact that Eglon had succeeded in subduing Israel brought to mind the fact that King Balak of Moab had failed to do so when he tried to hire the northern Mesopotamian prophet Balaam to curse Israel so he could be victorious over them (Num. 22–24). It is true God had forbidden the Israelites to encroach on Moabite lands (Deut. 2:8–9) when Israel wanted to cross through to go over the Jordan to the land God was giving them.

However, Eglon did not appear to be aware of the fact that his rise in dominating Israel was due to God's work and not attributable to any of his own efforts! It was the Lord who had "strengthened" Eglon's hand (3:12b), even though he may have thought he had independently forged an alliance with the Ammonites and Amalekites as he attacked Israel and occupied the "City of Palms" (cf. 1:16). The "City of Palms" was a Palestinian base, or perhaps his summer residence in the Jordan Valley, from which he exercised his rule over Israel and his own country of Moab. Apparently, King Eglon was unaware that Joshua had cursed the city of Jericho (Josh. 6:26), or that his occupation of that city represented an outright defiance of God and a disregard for the curse Israel had invoked against this city.

Eglon, despite ruling over Israel for 18 years, is treated in this text as a somewhat comical character, if not a buffoon. His name as given by the Israelites has wordplay: Hebrew `eglon seems to be a diminutive form of `egel, "bull, calf." Often Israelites used -on in names to mark a diminutive usage. But it could also be a play on `agol, "round, rotund." Judges 3:17 identifies him as an "extremely fat man." This assessment of his overall weight and person is confirmed in vv. 20–22 with the notation that when Ehud stabbed him with his homemade sword, Eglon's fat wrapped around the sword and Ehud could not retrieve his weapon. But in contrast to Eglon, the Moabite soldiers were "all vigorous and strong [men]."

The character of Judge Ehud, who was called by God to be Israel's new deliverer from the Moabite oppression, is nevertheless problematic. There is no question that to Israel he was a hero, but to the Moabites he was regarded as a terrorist and a villain. Ehud was clever when he concealed the fact that as a Benjamite he was left-handed and so hid his homemade sword on his right thigh under his clothing (3:16). Thus, one may admire the deceptive trick he pulled on the somewhat dimwitted King Eglon, but there are no grounds for condoning his treachery. The judgment of Phillips P. Elliott is thought-provoking:

> By even the most elementary standard of Ethics, [Ehud's] deception of Eglon stand condemned. Passages like this cause consternation and questioning.[1]

The narrative is totally silent on the means Ehud used in delivering Israel, even though Ehud was definitely called to rescue Israel from the eighteen years of servitude to Moab. Ehud operated according to the world's standards when he acted opportunistically and violently in bringing an end to those

---

1. Phillips P. Elliott, *Interpreter's Bible Commentary, Vol. II* (1952), 708, 711.

years of overlordship by the Moabites. Ehud was able to bring about peace for Israel over the next 80 years as Moab was made subject to Israel.

By Preparing the Way for a Deliverer – 3:12–14

Israel again did evil in the eyes of the Lord, so he sold them into the hand of Eglon, king of Moab. Eglon was able to do this because he rallied the troops of the Ammonites and the Amalekites to join him in attacking Israel (3:12–13). Thus, Scripture warns us that adopting evil as our way of life invites the hostile forces around us to be used of God to bring us back to our senses and to walking according to his divine word. The believing body in any age is weakened by its constant practice of sin, thus making it easy for the pagan forces in our world and day to capture us and take ground from under our feet! This is why Jericho was now being occupied by Eglon as his headquarters in the Jordan Valley for some 18 years (3:14).

After conquering the city, Eglon apparently did not know Jericho had been cursed by Joshua (Josh. 6:26). But he still placed his headquarters there, and if Josephus is accurate, Eglon erected fortifications and his residence there as he could obtain command over the fords at the crossing of the Jordan close to that point. Thus, he had easy communication with his home country of Moab, as well as control over preventing Israel's tribes on the east and west side of the river, to join forces in helping one another by stationing himself between the tribes living on either side of the Jordan!

Israel had neglected their Lord for eighteen years, and now their Lord would neglect them, for their sin had made them servants of Moab instead of being servants of God.

By Granting the Oppressed People a Deliverer – 3:15–23

Surprisingly, without any notice of repentance or a change of heart on the part of Israel, they "cried out to the LORD, and the LORD raised up a deliverer, Ehud, the son of Gera." If this is not an example of the mercy and grace of God, it is hard to find an even more telling example of how patient and loving our Lord is to us despite our tendency to sin.

Ehud was chosen from the tribe of Benjamin, who were famous for being left-handed, especially in the use of their weapons. (How that relates to their being named Benjamites, i.e., son[s] of [my] right hand," is unclear.) Ehud made a double-edged dagger about 15 to 18" long (*gomer*, 3:16, the only usage of this word in the Old Testament). Presumably, it was a word used for the short cubit, which measured 17.49 inches. A few others said it was 2/3 of a cubit, but there is no verification of either.

Ehud hid this dagger on his right thigh, under his clothing; of course it could easily be drawn by his left hand. Had Ehud been frisked upon entering the Moabite palace, they would have run their hand over his left thigh, thinking he was right-handed!

After Ehud had ended his presentation of what was likely the annual offering, the king sent away all the persons who had carried the offering from his throne room. It was not unusual for a fairly large number of persons to be used on such an occasion to increase the gifts' ostentatiousness and pompously display the taxes they were bringing.

However, soon after Ehud had left Jericho and had come to the place known as the "quarries," near Gilgal where Israel had made their first encampment after crossing the Jordan. These "quarries" in Hebrew were known as the *pesilim*, from the root meaning "to cut out, to carve, sculpted images." The Moabites' choice of such a spot for carving out their idols in these quarries must have been in contempt for Israel's worship of God. This may have been what stirred Ehud's indignation when he got the call from God to deliver Israel from the Moabites and their co-belligerents. Ehud returned to the Moabite king's palace, saying, "I have a secret message for you" (3:19). The Hebrew words used here were *debar seter*, "a word of secrecy or concealment." Moreover, it this was a "word from God" (3:20), then Eglon was exceedingly interested, vain as he was.

With that, Eglon once more cleared the room of all others, including guards and counselors, leaving him exposed and vulnerable. Ehud likely counted on this man's stupidity and weaknesses; if so, he certainly guessed correctly. The king urged Ehud to be quiet until the room was empty.

Scripture doesn't eulogize Ehud's conduct. Some praise Brutus' stabbing of Caesar; Brutus tried to justify his actions by stating he was ridding the country of a tyrant. But on what grounds then would Ehud vindicate his actions? Most will say that his grounds were that God had raised him up as a savior of the country. But did that mean any means he used would be accepted in the sight of God? Remember, the Bible makes no comment on how Ehud took out Eglon.

At first Ehud said he had a secret message, but later he said he had a word from God. Ehud meant that the dagger he had concealed was itself that word, but vain Eglon thought he was going to get some word from on high about his administration. Sensing the solemnity of the situation, Eglon rose from his throne, no doubt with great effort due to his overweight corpulence, only to have Ehud surprisingly rush up the stairs with a dagger in hand, the very one he had just retrieved from his right thigh, which he then thrust into Eglon's belly. The fat closed around his weapon, making it impossible to retrieve his homemade sword. There was no time to try to withdraw it, and even if he could, how would he clean the blade off and not get blood all over himself? Ehud had to leave no telltale signs in case he happened to run into any palace personnel on his way out.

Then the assassin quickly left the throne room through the porch and locked the doors behind him to the parlor, so that he could gain more time for his escape (3:23). Meanwhile, his servants reasoned that King Eglon was using the "cool room," or as the Bible's euphemistic expression puts it, "he [was]cover[ing] his feet," i.e., "he was relieving himself" (3:24). The cool room was the name sometimes used for the bathroom in Egyptian, so that might be its meaning here.

When Eglon fell from the stabbing in his belly and expired, apparently his bowels relaxed and discharged their contents all over the throne (3:22b). The Septuagint omits these words entirely, while a few argue that this Hebrew word *happarshedonah* refers to some type of "hole" or an architectural loop-hole through which the assassin escaped.

By Providing Time for an Escape – 3:24–27

Eglon's servants returned to the door of the throne room from their coffee break, only to find that the doors to the parlor were locked! (3:24) These lackies at first supposed the king was using the facilities, but when the doors remained shut over a longer period than they thought reasonable, they began to feel ashamed over the extended delay. So, the servants and guards finally got up enough nerve to locate the key to open the parlor doors, whereupon they discovered their king had fallen down dead (3:25).

While all of this was going on at the summer palace in Jericho, Ehud made a clean escape as the palace servants dilly-dallied at the locked door for an extended time. Ehud went beyond the quarries until he came to Seirah, a town near Gilgal. When he arrived there, he summoned the Israelites in the mountain of Ephraim to gather for battle by sounding his ram's horn (*shophar*, 3:27). Ehud led them from the mount of Ephraim to meet the Moabites, who by this time were now attempting to cross the Jordan from the environs of Jericho back to the safety of the eastern side of the Jordan and their homes in Moab.

By Gathering a Following Who Will Follow Him Into Battle – 3:28–30

The story of Ehud's assassination of Eglon must have spread like a brush fire. Ehud's word to these Ephraimites was: "Follow me, for the LORD has given Moab, your enemy, into your hands" (3:28). Now for the first time since v. 15, the Lord is the subject of the verb. Surely the death of this king would present a leadership vacuum and a tremendous amount of uncertainty and pandemonium in Moab. Ehud recognized that this was a favorable time, so he had better act swiftly if he was to take the advantage that was his in this moment in history, especially if he was going to be able to cast off completely the Moabite oppression of Israel.

Ehud was smart enough to secure the fords of the Jordan near the river's entrance to the Dead Sea, where he also set a strong guard against those who were trying to get in contact between the Moabites located west of the Jordan and those east of the river in Moab. Ehud cut off any and all communication between the two Moabites forces as he drove a wedge between the two parts of the Moabite contingent. Thus, no reinforcements were able to cross the Jordan to help those isolated in Jericho.

Ehud managed a victory that included 10,000 Moabite casualties. The health of these Moabite warriors was outstanding, for they "all [were] vigorous and strong" (3:29), which hardly describes an emaciated defeated army of Moab. The Moabite army was not at all corpulent and overweight like their leader, Eglon. Moreover, on that day, "Moab was made subject to Israel, and the land had peace for 80 years," a time of tranquility that lasted almost a full century! (3:30). This extended period of time would give Israel an opportunity to secure their hold on the land God had given to them. But it would also provide them with a time to turn to the Lord and to fellowship with him in the commands he had left for them to live by.

A curious note is added to the judgeship of Ehud in Judges 3:31: "After Ehud came Shamgar son of Anat." But many questions pop up as a result of this insertion. For example, the name Shamgar has four consonants—"sh-m-g-r." As similar forms to this name appear in the Nuzi texts, Shamgar is likely a Hurrian name. Equally puzzling is that he is the "son of Anat." In Canaanite mythology, Anat is the consort of Baal, the goddess of war, whose reputation extended far beyond Palestine. Some say instead that this meant Shamgar was a "member/native of the town of Anath" in Galilee.

Furthermore, Shamgar was not called a judge/ruler of his people as the other men listed in the book of Judges; instead, it is said that he "saved Israel" (Hebrew, *hoshia`*), which places him among the "saviors" of the nation. Shamgar did this work of saving by using an "ox-goad" (*malmad*) to kill 600 Philistines. The goad or prod was used to train and control cattle. It was made of hardwood and possibly tipped with an iron point. So can the brevity of this note in Scripture be explained by the fact that he was not an Israelite, but a foreigner? If so, where was the leadership taken in Israel to take care of these Philistines?

Conclusions

1. Were Ehud's deceptive tactics in any way approved by God even though he had been called by God to deliver Israel from the hand of Moab?

2. The king of Moab invited the Ammonites and Amalekites to join him in subjugating Israel for 18 years.

3. Ehud delivers the tribute from Israel with a Jewish retinue to Eglon's headquarters in Jericho, but then returns to this summer palace by himself.

4. Shamgar saved Israel by slaying 600 Philistines with an ox-goad.

Lesson 4

Judges Deborah and Barak
Conquer King Jabin of Hazor
Judges 4:1–24; 5:1–31

Judges 4 and 5 are unusual in that they provide two records of a single event, one in a prose form (chapter 4) and the other in a poetic format (chapter 5), yet both the poem and narrative show they both had access to the same data. Scholars generally consider the poetic form the older, and thus the original form in which the event was cast, though that is usually a matter of speculation unless this claim is supported by textual evidence.

God Allows Us to Suffer Oppression to Soften Our Hearts – 4:1–3

It seems many of the cities Joshua had destroyed in his day were subsequently rebuilt and refortified as centers of Canaanite opposition and resistance. Judge Shamgar had cleared out for Israel the Philistine border on the southwestern seacoast of the Mediterranean, but the Canaanites swept into the land that Israel had failed to occupy and had instead busied themselves just as the Gentiles had done who were living in Harosheth near the mouth of the Kishon wadi in the northwest corner of Esdraelon/Jezreel Valley; i.e., they had occupied themselves with forging more chariots of iron.

Jabin was the king of Hazor, a city located some four miles southwest of the Lake Huleh area and ten miles northwest of the Sea of Galilee, in the territory assigned to the tribe of Naphtali. This city was given the title of "the head of all those kingdoms" (Josh. 11:1, 10–11; 12:19; 19:36). The name "Jabin" actually may have been a hereditary title used (like "Pharaoh") by successive kings, rather than a personal name. The city over which that king, "Jabin," ruled was large with an estimated population of some 40,000 (whereas Jericho is estimated to have merely around 1500 persons at around the same time). Moreover, Hazor covered some 200 acres (compared to the city of Megiddo, which covered not even 20), but Joshua had burnt the city of Hazor with fire almost a century prior to the event narrated here in Judges. In light of such an enormous population and huge acreage for those times, it is no wonder Jabin is often said to have been a king of Canaan, for the surrounding cities were somehow affiliated with him and under his oversight as well (4:2, 23, 24).

The commander of Jabin's army was Captain Sisera, who made his headquarters at Haroshet Haggoyim. He functioned as the military leader of Jabin's combined armies. The Lord would choose Barak under Deborah to lead Israel's armies. He came from the town of Kedesh-Naphtali (4:6), which may be the same as Kedesh, some 12 miles north of Hazor.

As usual, "the sons of Israel … had done evil in the sight of the LORD" (4:1), so the Lord "sold them into the hand of Jabin king of Canaan, who reigned in Hazor, whose captain of his army was Sisera, who lived, as already mentioned in "Harosheth of the Gentiles" (4:2). As a result of Israel's moral failure, "they cried out to the LORD; for [Sisera] had nine hundred chariots of iron and cruelly oppressed the Israelites for twenty years" (4:3). Israel cried for relief from this mighty warrior.

Our God Sometimes Uses Women to Lead Us – 4:4–14

Deborah, whose name means "[honey]-bee," is described first as a "prophetess," which placed her on par with other women prophets such as: Miriam (Exod. 15:20), Huldah (2 Kgs. 22:14), the prophet Isaiah's unnamed wife, who also was identified as a "prophet" (Isa. 8:3), Anna (Luke 2:36), and the four unmarried daughters of Philip the Evangelist (Acts 21:9), including the wife of a man called Lappidoth, whose name is said to mean "torches." There is also Noadiah, but she was a false prophetess (Neh. 6:14).

At the time, Deborah "was leading Israel" as she also held forth in a judicial court under a palm tree in an unnamed town between Ramah and Bethel in the southern part of the tribe of Ephraim, some 50 miles south of where the ensuing battle between Barak and Sisera would take place in the Jezreel Valley (4:5). The Israelites seemed to have been in the habit of going to Deborah to resolve the types of disputes they had with each other.

Deborah summoned Barak (whose name means "lightning") the son of Abinoam, who was in Kedesh of Naphtali with the following message: "The LORD of Israel commands you: 'Go, take with you 10,000 men of Naphtali and Zebulun and lead them up to Mount Tabor. I will lead Sisera, the commander of Jabin's army, with his chariots and his troops to the Kishon River and give him into your hands'" (4:6–7). It does not appear that Barak had had such a call from God previously.

Now Mount Tabor rose out of the plain of Jezreel to some 1843 feet above sea level in a distinctive conical shape with rather steep slopes to its sides and was situated in the northeast corner of the Jezreel Valley. On this mountain Barak could be sure he was in a safe place from the operation of Sisera's iron chariots. But even with this empirical evidence and a divine assurance, Barak was not all that certain he wanted to do this. So he said, "If you [Deborah] go with me, I will go, but if you don't go with me, I won't go" (4:8). Deborah was already recognized as a "prophet" (*'ishshah nebi'ah*, "a woman, a prophet"); thus, her presence alongside Barak was an assurance of the divine presence to him.

Barak was aware of the kinds of resources (chariots) that were available to Sisera, whose army dominated the Esdraelon Plain/Jezreel Valley. Its geography cut the northern tribes of Israel off from those in the south, for the Plain of Esdraelon tended to divide the country into two main parts as it stretched east-west across the middle of Canaan! Still, God had given Barak a good place to go to on Mount Tabor, where Sisera and his chariots would be totally ineffective in the hill country. The question on the hearts and minds of Israel was: Who was Sisera in comparison to God?

Fortunately, Deborah agreed to go with Barak, but because he had exhibited so little personal faith (his name meant "lightning," but he showed no "flash" of leadership or accompanying "brilliance"), she informed him that because he had hidden behind her skirts ("I will go *if* you go"), "the honor will not be yours, for the LORD will deliver Sisera into the hands of a woman" (4:9)—who will turn out to be Jael.

In a parenthetical note, v. 11 says Heber, who had hailed from the family tribe called the Kenites, a group from which the woman who would be the real hero of this story, named Jael (4:17) would come. This is the group who also claimed to be descended from Hobab, Moses' father-in-law, who pitched his tent near the great tree in Zaanannim near Kadesh.

Our God Routs Our Enemies – 4:15–16

The Lord caused Sisera's troops and entire fleet of iron chariots to panic before Barak as confusion and disorder spread quickly through the ranks. What had happened may be gathered from the poem in 5:19–22. There the "waters of Megiddo" and the heavens come into the picture in the poem: "The river Kishon [which flows somewhat close-by the city of Megiddo] swept them away in the overflowing age-old river called the river Kishon." No doubt with a downpour of rain and hail, it left the banks of the Kishon River overflowing on the land so the iron chariots were no help. As they got bogged down in the mud, muck and mire, they became a hindrance, to say the least. Some of the chariots were able to make it to Harosheth of the Gentiles (4:16), but Barak chased after them all the way until they all fell by the edge of the sword, so that not a man was left.

No wonder, then, that Captain Sisera, overtaken by this critical turn in the nasty weather conditions, with the wind howling as well, was left in the driving rain to face these warriors. But most of the chariots were bogged down in the mud, along with his army sloshing along as best they could in the rain-soaked Jezreel Valley, which lay in front of Mount Tabor. What other option was left to Sisera than to abandon his prized but useless ivory-and-iron chariot as he "leap[ed]" (*yarad*, "to go down") from it and fled on foot to seek refuge as best he could. Meanwhile, Barak pursued those chariots still able to maneuver somewhat in the flooded fighting valley that ran alongside the Kishon River across the Jezreel Valley.

Our God Can Deliver Us Without Approving of the Means Used – 4:17-24

Sisera knew where he must go, for King Jabin was on friendly terms with Heber the Kenite, who just happened to be the husband of Jael, whose name means "mountain goat." Sisera felt he would be safe there, but when Sisera came toward Jael's tent, Jael went out to meet Sisera and urged him to come into her tent and not be afraid (4:18). Sisera accepted the invitation. Jael, acting like a good hostess, covered him with a blanket.

Once inside Sisera asked for a little water to quench his thirst, for he apparently had been on the run for a good distance by now (4:19). But Jael was even more generous, for instead she opened a "skin of milk" and gave him curds to drink—she "milked" this situation for all it was worth!

Then Sisera ordered her to stand watch at the door and if anyone came by inquiring if he or any other man might have come by her tent, she was to deny there was any such man there (4:20). Then, with brutal detail, Jael, now identified as "Heber's wife," took a "tent peg" (*yetad ha'ohel*) and a "mallet" as she quietly snuck up on resting Sisera, and she drove the tent peg into his skull (*raqqah*), pinning his head to the ground of her tent. Apparently, Sisera, exhausted from what he had been through, had already collapsed into a dead sleep! He died at once as Jael nailed her victim.

Such action may raise the question about the practice of prevarication or in some homes, where it is not an infrequent practice to instruct family members to say the parent is "in the shower" or some other such lie when they actually were away and the children were home alone. If children are taught to lie for others, they may be liable to do it for themselves as well!

After Jael had completed her mallet act, Barak, leader of the Israelite forces appeared at Jael's tent now in search of Sisera (4:22). Jael came out to him and said, "Come, and I will show you the man you are looking for." When Barak came into her tent, Sisera lay dead, nailed to the dirt floor with the tent peg still in place. So that is how God *subdued* Jabin, "king of Canaan" (the Hebrew word for "subdue," *kana'*, comes from the same root as the word for "Canaan," *kena 'an*, punning these words) by the hand of the children of Israel (4:23). God continued to prosper the work of Israel as they prevailed over Jabin until they finally destroyed him (4:24).

The Song of Deborah: A Poetic Celebration of Victory – 5:1–31

Deborah and Barak, the son of Abinoam, on that day of victory, sang a song of praise to the Lord for his deliverance from the forces of Jabin and Sisera (5:1). The verb is in the feminine form, thus again giving precedence to the woman, as was the case with Miriam and her song of victory (Num. 12:1). This may only mean that Deborah composed the song, while all Israel actually joined in singing it under the direction of her and Barak. This song probably was not sung about the same time as a victory ode over Sisera, for "on that day" may imply simply "about that time" rather the self-same day!

They praised the Lord for "breaking away the bonds" (para`, "to break away," "to let loose" or "freeing of freedoms") as the people asserted their freedom (5:2). Therefore, all kings and princes are to get ready to hear the prophetess begin her song of triumph. So the "kings" and "princes" were to listen as Deborah sang her song unto the Lord for the way he had delivered Israel (5:3). Deborah regarded herself as a feeble woman, yet she celebrated with all her might the way the Lord had overthrown Sisera and his troops. Then with a sudden poetic apostrophe, Deborah turned to address the Lord who had demonstrated his awesome power and might in the past on Israel's way out of Egypt through "Seir and the field of Edom" (5:4). These demonstrations of God's power and might saw, as it were, the heavens drop snow, the clouds drop water, and the mountains melt before the Lord (5:4–5). These became like the days of the judge "Shamgar the son of Anat," and the days of "Jael" when the highways were empty, because they were known for robbers who assaulted travelers (5:6).

Deborah presents her rise at this time to meet this challenge when Israel had faced such a great crisis. Not only did the populace seek the back roads instead of the robber-infested highways, but the villages were likewise deserted, for these villages had no protecting walls, as some of the cities in Israel had. Deborah refers to her call to rise up and lead Israel with the honorific title of "mother in Israel," whereas the actual deliverers of Israel were called the "fathers of Israel" (5:7).

With Deborah's rise to lead Israel, it was time for "new leaders" to take the offensive as war came to the gates of Israel's cities (5:8). Some 40,000 Israelites responded to the call to take up the battle, but not a spear or shield could normally be found among this Israeli army (5:8b).

Deborah expressed her admiration for those who offered themselves willingly and freely (5:9). She was especially thankful for the people's courage. She appealed to the rich who rode on tawny female donkeys, which were much preferred over the generic grays. A white donkey would have been extremely rare and have come from Arabia.[1] These donkey riders flaunted their status, dressing their donkeys with luxurious saddle blankets (5:10). The translation of v. 11 is difficult, but it seems to describe the excited conversations held by those who typically gathered at their favorite watering-holes, whether springs or wells! They talked about "the righteous acts of the LORD" and the "righteous acts of Israel's warriors" (5:11b).

Those righteous acts of the Lord are now recounted in vv. 11b–18, for just as v. 8 began with "Then," so does v. 11e. The people of Israel "went down against the gates," meaning the fortified cities of the Canaanites. Verse 12 increases in emotional intensity with a twofold summons to Deborah to rouse herself to action. Barak also receives such a call, but it is just to give a single summon to arise and lead his captives in captivity, while Deborah leads out in a song of victory, acting on her double summons (5:12). She recites the roll-call of Israel's warriors in vv. 14–18 from the tribes that showed up to help. She showed her disappointment, however, with those in Israel who did not respond, for the list can be broken down into three groups: the volunteers (vv. 14–15a), the resistors (vv. 15b–17), and finally the award-winners (v. 18).

To the Ephraimite tribe Deborah seems to give the most credit. This may have been the tribe she was from, and the Amalekites seemed to have settled among Benjamin. Next came the Benjamites, who because of their small size joined the Ephraimite tribe. Then came Makir, the oldest of Manasseh's sons, whose name often stands for the tribe of Manasseh (Gen. 50:23; Num. 27:1), who, with the tribe of Zebulun, were mustered for action with those who recorded the names of those who enlisted for the battle. Deborah called the men of Issachar "my princes" (5:15); their military service had inspired her, as did that of Barak, who descended from the slopes of Mount Tabor into the plain of Esdraelon to attack the Canaanites.

---

1. See the note in Daniel I. Block, *Judges: An Exegetical and Theological Exposition of Holy Scripture, Vol. 6* (1999), 228.

Among the resistors, however, was the tribe of Reuben, who gave serious reflection to joining Israel's forces in v. 16, but Deborah wondered why the Reubenites sat around campfires discussing the matter as musicians entertained them with shepherd pipes. Verse 17 adds the names of "Gilead" (which had settled on the east side of the Jordan in Transjordania between the Yarmuk River and the Wadi Heshbon in the south as the tribe of Gad), along with the names of Dan and Asher.

Those chosen for special honors by Deborah, however, were Zebulun and Naphtali, who had rushed fearlessly into the jaws of danger and death. The "high places of the field" seems to refer to Mount Tabor (5:18).

The actual battle between the army of Israel (under Deborah and Barak) and the Canaanites takes place in vv. 19–23. Since Hazor is expressly said to be the head of a number of petty principalities (Josh. 11:10), it is understandable why Judges 4 said the battle was against Jabin king of Hazor and Judges 5 says the "kings of Canaan in Taanach by the waters of Megiddo." The Wadi Kishon, of course, runs near Megiddo, which Sisera and his chariots had to cross to get to Barak during a great storm (5:19). It appears the heavenly forces likewise joined in that day, as the stars and the wind, thunder, lightning and rain did their part to make it hard for Sisera and his prized chariotry to be effective (5:20). In fact, some argue that this reference to the stars alludes to an eclipse near Megiddo in 1131 B.C.E.[2] The Kishon Wadi became an overflowing river that began near the eastern foot of Mount Tabor; after going westward through the Esdraelon Valley, it fell into the Mediterranean at the southeast corner of the Bay of Acre. The Kishon was turned into a mighty current, overflowing and softening the ground. Many of the chariots were swept away by this sudden deluge as the stallions reared up with frantic frenzy in the tumult of the thunder and lightning and the roar of the swift current (5:22–23).

This stanza of vv. 19–23 concludes with a messenger of God commanding that Meroz be cursed because it did not rally to the support

---

2. J. F. A. Sawyer, "From Heaven Fought the Stars," *Vetus Testamentum*, 1 (1981), 87–89.

against the Canaanites (5:23). Meroz is only mentioned in the Bible in this passage. As best as we can guess, it is located somewhere in the area around Mount Tabor's eastern side where Barak assembled his troops with Megiddo to the south of their assembly point (5:23).

Deborah's musical ode took an unexpected turn in vv. 24–27 as our attention is shifted from the armies fighting in the valley to the inside of the tent of Jael as a chance encounter takes place between Sisera and this woman Jael, the wife of Heber the Kenite, but one who now was known as "most blessed of tent-dwelling women" (5:24).

Once inside the safety of Jael's tent, Sisera asked for water, but Jael gave him the lordly dish of "curds" or "yogurt" (*hem'ah*) (5:25). Then Jael reached for the tent-peg, and with a mallet she drove the tent-peg through his skull as she pierced Sisera's temple. With that, Sisera fell dead at her feet (5:27). Jael drove the final stake for victory in this battle, and she was the one who had been predicted to win the credit for winning the battle.

This victory ode from Deborah concludes in vv. 28–31 with Sisera's mother depicted as a worried mother looking out the window and wondering why her son was taking so long and now delayed from his victorious return. Her consolation was not focused, however, on Sisera's victory, but it is centered instead on the victor's prizes of a slave or two for each warrior, a huge lot of captured many-colored garments, a load of splendid ornaments and a large assortment of attire for all (5:28).

Sisera's mother's "wise ladies" speculated on why he had been held up for such a long time, but his mother's thoughts were elsewhere. She thought perhaps the men each have taken a damsel or two for themselves, while Sisera himself had probably garnered a stash of needlework of various colors, for she imagined that some of the cloths would have colors on both sides bound for the necks of those who captured this loot (5:30).

Deborah ended her song by praying on the one hand that all of Israel's enemies would perish just as Sisera had experienced such a crushing fate, but she also prayed for all those who love God to shine like the sun with ever-increasing splendor, diffusing its light wherever it goes (5:31).

Conclusions

1. The battle is the Lord's despite who is employed or what instruments he may use—such as the weather, the flooded Wadi Kishon, the wife of an old relative of Moses named Heber, or a woman judge named Deborah!

2. God went ahead of Deborah and Barak to win the war just as he has gone ahead of us in many instances in our day.

3. Barak's hesitancy to fully obey the Lord unless Deborah went with him meant God would use two women, Deborah and Jael, to complete the job he originally had called Barak to do, just as it so often happens in our day on the mission field and elsewhere in Christian service.

4. When we pray "Thy kingdom come, thy will be done, on earth as it is in heaven," we ask God to intervene and to destroy the devil's work, along with every conspiracy against his divine work, until his kingdom comes in all its fullness.

5. God must either direct or permit all that happens on earth even if he does not always approve of all the means used to accomplish that work.

Lesson 5

The Lord Is With Judge
Gideon to Defeat the Midianites

Judges 6:1–40

Judge Gideon is given unusually extensive coverage in the book of Judges. Altogether there are 100 verses and three chapters (6–8) set aside for the life and leadership of this son of Joash. The deliverance God gave Israel through this man must have been pivotal to the people of Israel, for it is given an expansive narration detailing how God worked through him to send them deliverance from the Midianites. That Gideon's story will be told in an extended way can be seen right away as the first six verses are given at the start of chapter 6 to describe how God responded to this new apostasy among his people Israel (6:1b–5). Even though God's name is absent from 6:2–6b, v. 1b asserts his name by a pronoun: "He [God] gave them [Israel] into the hands of the Midianites." The hostile nations of Midian, Amalek and the sons of the East pulled off this act of thievery seven years in a row. They would descend on the land as thick as a locust infestation each year and steal the crops that were just ripening up and haul them off, along with all the animals they could take. It was outrageous!

Israel had been warned that this punishment was exactly what would happen if they transgressed God's covenant, for this is precisely what covenant-breakers could expect from God for their repeated disobedience:

> Day after day you will be oppressed and robbed, with no one to rescue you. ... Your ox will be slaughtered before your eyes, but you will eat none of it. Your donkey will be forcibly taken from you and will not be returned. Your sheep will be given to your enemies, and no one will rescue them. (Deut. 28: 29c, 31)

The principal agents of such divine judgment were the Midianites, but they were accompanied and aided by the Amalekites and the Easterners. The Midianites were a semi-nomadic people who lived in the Sinai Peninsula, but they also were direct relatives of the Israelites, from the line of Abraham through his second wife Keturah (Gen. 25:2–4). The Midianites were involved in the sale of Joseph to the Egyptians, but there was no direct word of divine judgment for the part Joseph's brothers played in this (Gen. 37:25–36), though Joseph himself later viewed the Midianites as agents of God's providence (Gen. 45:4–8; 50:19–20). There were times, however, when the Midianites were depicted in a positive light, as the time when they gave Moses a place to stay in Midian after he had fled from Pharaoh, because he had just killed an Egyptian. Eventually the Midianites also provided Moses with a wife, named Zipporah, meaning "Lady Bird," the daughter of Jethro, a Midianite priest (Exod. 2:15–22). What a beautiful story in which Moses, now residing on a Midianite ranch, marries "Lady Bird."

Moreover, Moses' father-in-law Jethro suggested a more efficient way of organizing help for Moses when he acted to give legal relief to Israelites. Moses' burden of meeting with each individual case must not rest totally on Moses' shoulders, advised Jethro (Exod. 18:15–27). Jethro gave Moses a plan that would distribute the load more equably.

There was, for example, the incident in Numbers 25:1–18 and 31:1–18 where Israel was coaxed by the people of Midian into worshiping Baal of Peor, but we will hold that story for a minute.

How then did Israel get out of this dilemma of losing their crops and cattle for seven years in a row? Let's look at this chapter in greater detail for the answer. What type of sin had Israel committed to provoke the judgment of God in such a painful way? This is the story that follows.

In the Impoverishment God Permits of Israel's Produce – 6:1–6

Israel tended to exhibit new ways of defecting from the Lord, so that is why a new judgment came. He had warned Israel that with the froward he would show himself froward, and with those who walked contrary to his word, he would walk contrary to them! That is what happened here!

Many of the Midianites had been cut off centuries ago by Moses, because of the brazen act of Zimri, from the tribe of Simeon in Israel, who took Kozbi, a Midianite, into his tent for a sexual act at the very moment all Israel was gathered in repentance for the same sin. Zimri and Kozbi thought what they were doing was nothing less than a religious act of worshiping the Midianite god Baal of Peor (Num. 25:1–18; 31:1–18). Now, many years later, the Midianites apparently wanted to retaliate for the way they had been so totally defeated so long ago, so they were joined by the Amalekites and the members of the East to attack Israel in each of the seven years in a row where they had pulled off a brazen robbery of the produce of Israel's land, leaving Israel to experience a famine!

So heavy was the hand of these three hostile and enemy forces on Israel each year that the Israelites were forced to take up residence in dens, caves and strongholds in the mountains to hide and retain a small portion of their food supplies, eking out a miserable existence for themselves.

Finally, Israel's misery got to such a point that they gave voice to it as they cried out to God for relief from the invaders. Israel had been brought low under God's judgment. Meanwhile, these marauding Bedouins seized all the herds and cattle Israel owned as they ravaged the land from north to south, all the way down to Gaza, occupied at times by the Philistines.

In the Accusations God Levels Against Israel and Us – 6:7–10

God's relief for Israel was to send a "prophet" to call them to repent (6:8). At first, some may wonder how in the world a prophet would remedy this situation, thinking this would be like sending a philosopher to help a stranded motorist. But their puzzlement over God sending a prophet was because they (and we) have too little confidence in the mighty power of the word of God. That's where Israel had gone wrong in the first place!

The prophet's message, however, came in the standard genre of a prophetic speech with its content coming from God. It included the following typical prophetic form or literary genre (6:8–10)...

It began with an introductory formula: "This is what the LORD, the God of Israel says." Then it rehearsed God's acts of grace: "I brought you up out of Egypt, out of the land of slavery. I delivered you from the hand of the Egyptians, and from the hand of all your oppressors. I drove them out before you and gave you their land." Next was a Reminder of the Lord's stipulations: "And I said to you, 'I am the LORD your God; you must not worship the gods of the Amorites, in whose land you live." And finally, this accusation: "But you have not listened to me."

Israel was told not to fear the gods of the Amorites, by which the Lord meant those of the land of Canaan, just as Israel had not feared former oppressors and opponents such as Sihon, Og, the men of Arad, or Balak. God had delivered Israel in the past and he could once again deliver them in the present situation and on into the future. Why then had Israel refused to obey God's voice (6:10c)? Did they pay no attention to history and to what God had done for them in the past? Were they hard of hearing?

In the Promises God Gives Israel and Us – 6:11–24

The call of Gideon and his rise to the task of delivering Israel is encompassed in a literary genre known as a "call narrative." Our passage has almost all the elements of a divine call: God and/or his messenger confronts Gideon with a call from heaven; we are introduced to the person God is calling for the task he has in mind, Gideon; there is a divine commission for the call, within which any objections are to be raised, but it all will be solidly backed up by God's words of reassurance; and the entire call might often be concluded with a "sign," which would act as an authentication or validation of that call.

It appears the Lord himself is meant by the title "an angel of the LORD" in v. 11, for in v. 14 he is spoken of as the "LORD" and in vv. 12 and 16, the Lord promises to "go with" the man he is calling, as that leader who will successfully strike down the Midianites.

The Lord, then, came and sat down under the oak tree in Ophrah that belonged to a man called "Joash" (a shortened form of "Jehoash," meaning "God is strong"), a man from the family of Abiezra, but a father who had a son named Gideon, whose name meant "hacker" or "hewer" (6:11b), a skill this son would soon need as he would be instructed by the Lord to destroy the altar erected to Baal on his father's property (6:25–27).

At the time of Gideon's call, he was "threshing wheat in a winepress to keep it from the Midianites," likely in a cave to conceal his work and its results (6:11d). The Abiezrites came from the tribe of Manasseh, which owned land on both sides of the Jordan (Josh. 17:2; 1 Chron. 17:8). In the case of Joash, however, his property was on the west side of the Jordan, possibly at the modern site of `Afulleh, in the Jezreel Valley.

God announced his presence to Gideon: "The LORD is with you, mighty warrior" (*gibbor hehayil*, "mighty warrior;" 6:12b). But Gideon protested:

> "But sir, If the LORD is with us, why has all this happened to us? Where are all his wonders that our fathers told us about when they said, 'Did not the LORD bring us up out of Egypt?" But now the LORD has abandoned us and put us in the hand of Midian" (6:13).

Gideon's response may not have been all that polite, for it may also have included some sarcasm. Gideon charged the Lord with abandoning his people Israel and giving them into the hands of the Midianites. He had some other objections as well; for example, he explained that his family was among the poorer people in the tribe of Manasseh and that he, Gideon, was regarded as the least in his family (6:15). But this was a false sense of modesty; his father Joash was a man of considerable wealth. Consider: Joash sponsored a Baal cult site on his property, including an Asherah image, and a temple fortress (6:25–26), thus Gideon used his apparent access to ten of his father's servants to help him tear down this altar (6:27). So how did he figure he was all that poor? Had Gideon ever stopped long enough to consider how God's grace had been keeping him alive, for our God "is rich in mercy" (Eph. 2:4) to help those who are dead in their sins and trespasses, even though we and Gideon are among those who are by nature are children of wrath? This same Lord had promised Moses that "[he] would be with [him]" (Exod. 3:12) as he had spoken the very same words to Joshua (Josh. 1:5). This also was God's promise to Gideon: "Surely I will be with you, and you shall smite the Midianites as one man" (6:18b).

Gideon pleaded with the Lord not to depart until he could bring to him an offering/meal (6:18a). Scholars debate whether this was a sacrifice or a "hospitality meal." The Hebrew here is *minchah*, a "meal offering" made of oil, flour, wine and bread. Perhaps it signified both ideas of a meal and an offering/sacrifice, for Gideon may have left it up to God to determine which it would be considered!

Gideon quickly went and made ready a young goat from his flock. Perhaps he stewed or boiled one part of the kid and roasted the other part, cutting the meat into small pieces and then strung them on a skewer, and presented them to the Lord in a dish called *kabab* along with unleavened bread. The broth he placed in a pot (6:19), all of which he brought to our Lord and presented while he was still seated under the Oak Tree where he had promised to stay until Gideon returned (6:18b).

When Gideon returned with the offering/meal for the "angel of the LORD," he was told to take the meat of the goat and the unleavened cakes and lay them on the nearby rock and then pour out the broth, presumably over the elements he had placed there (6:20). Then the Lord stretched out the end of the staff in his hand and touched the meat and the unleavened loaves of bread with it. Immediately fire arose from the rock, and the offering was consumed. With that, the angel of the Lord left Gideon's sight.

This act of setting the offering aflame with a fire from heaven was indeed a "sign" that this so-called "angel" was not a man who needed meat, nor an angel, but was the Lord himself, who also thereby demonstrated that this act showed God had accepted the sacrifice and that Gideon had found grace in the eyes of the Lord.

Though the "angel of the LORD" had a staff in his hand and may have seemed only a traveler, he did not walk with a staff as a man would, but he vanished as a spirit might in the flame of the fire (6:21). This must have scared the life out of Gideon, who declared he had seen God and therefore must die (6:22; Gen. 16:13; 32:30; Exod. 33:20). But the Lord assured him he would not die, for his peace would rest on him. Gideon built an altar to the Lord and named it "Jehovah-Shalom" (6:24). This altar in Ophrah of the Abiezrites was still in existence in the day when Judges was written.

In the Demands He Makes of Israel and Us – 6:25- 32

On the very same night as Gideon erected an altar unto the Lord, he was given two commands, one negative and the other positive. He was to destroy the false cult installation his father had erected for the community, which featured an altar to the pagan god Baal. And second, he was to "cut down" the Asherah pole. He was to "tear down" this cultic site using two of his father's bulls. Though translation after translation renders the Hebrew as "two bulls," only one seems to be used to tear down the altar, and that same bull was then sacrificed to the Lord after it had helped destroy the altar. The so-called first bull never appears in the narrative or is used in any way in this demolition project. The solution to this problem of "two bulls" is suggested by J. A. Emerton, who derives the Hebrew *hashsheni* not from the word for "second" [bull] but from a root meaning "to be exalted, of high rank," i.e., his father's "prime/prize bull" (6:25).[1]

Asherah was Baal's female counterpart, normally depicted with exaggerated female parts; this wooden image was carved on a tree near a cult altar; thus, to get rid of it, Asherah must be "cut down." Gideon was to build an altar to the Lord on this pagan site, which is called a "stronghold" or (in the NIV) on a "bluff." With this divine directive, Gideon was instructed to build an altar to the Lord by reclaiming the site for the Lord. He was to offer his father's prize bull, using the wood from the cut-down-Asherah image for the fire to fuel the sacrifice (6:26).

This is just what Gideon did; he tore down the altar of Baal with his father's prize seven-year-old-bull and he cut down the Asherah tree-pole. Then he offered to the Lord the bull he had used to "bull-doze" the

---

1. J. A. Emerton, "The 'Second Bull' in Judges 6:25-28," *Erez Israel,* 14 (1978): 52.

Asherah image with the help of the ten of his father's servants, whom he had awakened to help (6:27). This was done during the night, as Gideon feared his father's household and the men of the city (6:27d).

The next morning the men of that town, who no doubt had stopped off at Joash's place for a little Baal morning worship time, were shocked to death by what they beheld: their beloved altar to Baal was smashed and lay in ruins, for someone had destroyed Baal's altar and had cut down the Asherah image. In fact, the ashes of Joash's prize seven-year-old-bull were lying on a newly constructed altar dedicated to God! (6:28) The natural question on everyone's lips was: "Who did this?" (6:29) Quickly they had their answer: It was none other than Joash's own son Gideon who had destroyed their religious site and the object of their worship, Baal (6:29b).

So the men of Ophrah ordered Joash: "Bring out [of your house] your son, [for] he must die" (6:30). But Joash wisely replied to his neighbors:

> "Are you going to plead [Hebrew, *rib*, meaning "to stand up in defense of someone] Baal's cause? Are you trying to save him [Baal]? Whoever fights for him shall be put to death by morning! If Baal really is a god, he can defend himself when someone breaks down his altar" (6: 31).

Apparently, Joash himself had been experiencing serious doubts about the validity of the worship of Baal; now that his son was on trial, he showed little or no regard for the desecrated altar, nor did he exhibit any special concern over the loss of his prize bull! Moreover, God's law specifically called the worship of an idol like Baal a capital offense, but the wicked men of Ophrah impudently inverted this and made a penalty for the worshipers of God who denied Baal's legitimacy! Here were some early signs of the current "cancel culture"!

As a result of Gideon's actions, "he was called" (not by Joash, but by others in Ophrah) Jerubbaal. As they explained, it meant: "Let Baal plead against him," playing on *rib*, the Hebrew word for "plead" (6:32).

In the Assurances God Piles Up for Israel and Us – 6:33–40

Once again the Midianites and their allies crossed the Jordan and camped in the fertile Valley of Jezreel in Israel (6:33). But on this occasion "the Spirit of the LORD came upon Gideon" and filled him with great courage, zeal and wisdom (6:34). More literally, this phrase means "The Spirit of the LORD clothed himself with Gideon." The same verb is used in 1 Chron. 12:18; 2 Chron. 24:20. As such, Gideon became an extension of the Lord, for he was indwelt by the Holy Spirit.

Gripped by the Spirit of God, Gideon was ready for the work God was calling him to. Gideon caused the trumpets (*shophar*, "ram's horn) to be blown, a call for Jewish volunteers to come to help him, just as the judge Ehud had given the same trumpet alert to summon workers (3:27).

The first to respond were the men of Abiezer, Gideon's own hometown, the very same persons who had just called for his death. No doubt this reversal was a great encouragement to Gideon. But for some, this about-face raises this question: Why were they so impressed that they went from arguing he should die (for destroying the altar) to being the first to respond to his call to arms? Was it Gideon's courage they suddenly saw? The answer is that the "Spirit of the LORD had clothed Gideon."

Along with the tribe of Manasseh, Gideon's own tribe, help also came from the tribes of Asher, Zebulun and Naphtali to answer his call, all of whom lived fairly close to the Jezreel Valley and were near to Manasseh. So they too had felt the pressure of these dreadful Midianite attacks over the years (6:35). If their neighbor Manasseh had been overrun by the Midianites' thievery, then it stood to reason that their turn would be next, so they cheerfully responded. To the south of Manasseh was the tribe of Ephraim, who were not invited to help; this led the Ephraimites to raise loud recriminations against Gideon later in chapter 8 of Judges.

Now that Gideon was promised the Spirit of God and he was surrounded by a sizable army of neighboring tribes, he still hesitated. He wanted another sign from God, but this is not a text on how mortals can likewise determine the will of God in our day, for Gideon already knew

God wanted him to go into battle, just as the Lord had stated in verse 16 that "I will be with you, and you will strike down all the Midianites together." So, what was the problem? Why was he still hesitating?

Gideon proposed a test in which he would put outside overnight on the ground a fleece or a shearing of wool (*nizzat*, from *nazaz*, "to shear"). If the Lord would make this fleece wet while the surrounding ground was dry, then he would know he was to deliver Israel. In the morning, Gideon wrung a bowl of water from the fleece while the land around it remained dry. That should have satisfied him, but he was refusing not only a direct word from God, but now also the very sign he had just requested. It seemed very much like he was trying just to get out of this one way or another.

Gideon did apologize to God and asked that his reluctance not stir up God's anger, but Gideon wanted the sign reversed. Yes, this second sign was even more extraordinary than the first. It would have been natural for the woolen fleece to absorb any moisture from the air, but to now ask "Elohim" to make the fleece dry and the ground dew-covered made it seem as if he were trying to manipulate God. But remarkably, once more God patiently worked with him and made no complaint against Gideon. The fleece was perfectly dry, and the ground was soaked and heavy with dew. God had answered all Gideon's objections; he should be ready to go!

Conclusions

1. Israel sinned once more before God, so he brought the Midianites, the Amalekites and the members of the East as enemies against Israel.

2. The Lord sent a prophet to the people of Israel with a word from God, which promised that the Lord would deliver Israel from their enemies if his prophet would trust him.

3. The second person of the Trinity appearing as the "Angel of the LORD" came to the village of Ophrah, and he sat down under an oak tree that belonged to Gideon's father Joash, where Gideon and Joash were threshing wheat in a winepress located in a cave.

4. The Lord called Gideon a "mighty man of valor" and showed him that he would save the Israelites from Midian and his allies.

5. Gideon asked the Angel of the LORD to stay while he prepared a young goat, unleavened bread and broth for him. When Gideon served it, the Angel of the LORD put the end of his staff on the food and departed in the fire that rose out of the rock to consume the food.

6. Gideon built an altar to the Lord and named it Jehovah-Shalom. On that same night, Gideon, with the help of ten of his father's servants, tore down the Baal altar, cut down the Asherah pole and offered the bull he had used as a sacrifice to the Lord.

7. The Spirit of the LORD clothed Gideon as the men of the nearby Israelite tribes responded to attack Midian and all his allied hosts after God confirmed this call by two signs involving the woolen fleece.

Lesson 6

Gideon Defeats the Midianite Coalition
Judges 7:1–25; 8:1–35

Gideon, now renamed "Jerubbaal," got up early in the morning and made camp at last, with his 32,000 troops, at the "Spring of Harod," just five miles south of the Midianite camp, where Midian's some 135,000 made camp at the base of Mount Moreh, near the eastern end of the Valley of Jezreel/Esdraelon. The spring's name, "Harod," means "trembling" or terror"—which is exactly what overcame the Midianites. It was at the base of the mountains of Gilboa. Mount Moreh on the Gilboa range was named "Hill of the Archers," which may have referred to a later battle, in which the Philistine archers would kill King Saul at this spot (1 Sam. 31:3). If this is true, then Judges may have been written after the battle we are about to see.

Though Gideon faced a huge Midianite force well over four times the number of his own soldiers, the Lord announced to Gideon that, as a matter of fact, he already had too many troops with him, for God the great warrior to hand over the Midianite forces to him in victory. He had to *reduce* his army size! This, then, is the setting for this chapter.

By Reducing the Number of Those Unfit for Battle – 7:1–8

It is clear that the reason the Lord wanted the number of soldiers in Gideon's ranks reduced was to keep Israel from being downright boastful and from claiming that the victory over these raiding poachers on their land was because of this army's human initiative (7:2). One of the earlier Psalms would underline this truth for Israel to use in all her later history:

With your hand you drove out the nations
You crushed the peoples,
And made our ancestors flourish.

It was not by their sword that they won the land,
Nor did their arm bring them victory;
It was your right hand [LORD], your arm,
And the light of your face, for you loved them. (Psalm 44:2–3)

Gideon obeyed God's command to reduce the number of his forces, so 22,000 departed, leaving a mere 10,000 to face at least 135,000 hostile foes. But in God's estimation, Gideon still had too many fighters, so before the battle was engaged, he was to bring them down Harod's Spring, where the Lord would test them (7:4a). Our Lord's point was that only his presence, not the number of fighters, could assure them of success. Moreover, God often works best through a handful of men who really trust him and are dedicated to obeying his instructions. This must have tried Gideon's soul enormously, for he had already seen two-thirds of his recruits melt away before the battle. Perhaps he could have justified the loss of the first reduction on the grounds that maybe it was better these men leave to improve the troops' morale. Whoever, then, was "fearful" or "afraid" could be excused by departing from the fight on Mount Gilead on the east side of the Jordan.[1] But a second reduction showed him that this battle would not be a contest of human strength; it would be about the power of God to do with a few what others wanted to do with many!

Gideon brought his army to the spring. "The LORD told him, 'Separate those who lap the water with their tongues as a dog laps from those who kneel to drink'" (7:5). Some got on their knees and drank from cupped hands, while others lapped up like dogs. Interestingly, God told Gideon to keep the 'lappers' and send home the others. Wouldn't those who knelt be more alert if enemy action arose, while the 300 (who likely laid on the banks) would not be in a position for quick action? That is the point: God has deliberately not used a vast army nor the best

---

1. Mount Gilead was on the east side of Jordan, whereas Gideon was on the west side. There is no evidence that this was a misreading of "Gilead" as "Gilboa." Rather, a selection of replacement men would be made from the men of Mount Gilead from the Abiezrites among whom Gideon dwelt.

men; *he* will rout the enemy; the victory will be *his*, not the Midianites', and they will not be able to boast.

By Predicting Success for the Fainthearted – 7:9–15a

The army remained with the camp of Midian to the north by the hill of Moreh (7:8b). That night, the Lord told Gideon that if he still was afraid he might not be successful, he was to sneak down into the camp of Midian at night and he would hear there how God would deliver Midian into his hand (7:9). If he feared to go down to that camp by himself, he was to take his servant Purah with (7:10). So, with Purah at his side, what the two of them heard would calm some of their fears and would help confirm some of Gideon's statements to his 300 fighters when they returned to the camp.

Meanwhile, the Midianites and the Amalekites, along with the children of the east, were spread out in the Jezreel Valley vast as grasshoppers along with innumerable camels (7:12). Gideon was promised that as he and his servant approached the Midianite camp, they would hear what those there said (7:11). Sure enough, Gideon stealthily arrived in time to hear a man in one tent telling his dream to a friend (7:13). In the dream, he saw a loaf of barley-bread tumble down into the Midianite camp, for the Midianites were camped to the north of Gideon on Mount Moreh, while the enemy was stationed in the valley below. In the dream, the loaf struck the Midianite tent with such force that it overturned and collapsed (7:13). Had this object been a huge stone, it might not have created any unusual admiration, but this was a lowly loaf of barley-bread! (7:13). Indeed, this was not just any loaf; it was barley, the food that more and more came to be used mainly by the poor people in their midst, among their convicts, and by their beasts, which later was being slowly replaced by loaves of wheat. So, Gideon himself was associated with what was insignificant and lowly. This loaf rolled into "a tent"; the Hebrew again uses the collective singular for a plural.

Upon hearing this dream, another Midianite in that same enemy tent concluded that it meant this was nothing less than the sword of Gideon and of the Lord. Gideon could not have been more encouraged (7:14).

This interpreter also concluded that God had delivered Midian into Gideon's hand (7:14b). Wow! What a confirmation of God's call! More, when Gideon heard what was related in this dream and its "interpretation" (literally *shibro*, "the breaking thereof") given it, he worshiped the Lord and returned to the Israelite camp with thanks to God (7:15). Gideon was not troubled that he had been called a loaf of poor barley-bread, for he had the divine promise that his forces would roll down the hill of Moreh and burst into the tents of Midian and leave them distraught and in pieces!

By Standing Still and Watching God Work – 7:15a–25

Gideon returned and addressed his 300 men: "Arise, the LORD has delivered the Midianite camp into your hands" (7:15b). He laid out a simple strategy: He'd divide the 300 men into three companies so they could encircle the entire Midianite camp and thus appear to be a larger force than they actually were (7:16a). Each soldier was given a trumpet and an earthenware pitcher with a torch hidden inside (7:16b). Then Gideon instructed:

> "Watch me," he told them. "Follow my lead. When I get to the edge of the camp, do exactly as I do. When I and all who are with me blow our trumpets, then from all around the camp blow yours and shout, 'For the LORD and for Gideon!'" (7:17–18)

Then the three platoons circled the Midianite camp, and when the signal was given, the troops blew their trumpets, smashed their pitchers and stood in place holding high their flaming torches. The blasting of the horns must have awakened all in the camp, who had just settled down for a good night's sleep at the beginning of the middle watch (7:19). The middle watch was a little after midnight, for the Hebrews divided the night into three watches. But for those who had been suddenly awakened by such a racket, just as most had sunk into deepest slumber, were thrown into confusion stirred up much havoc and commotion in the darkness.

The panic that broke out among the Midianites caused them to be unable to distinguish between friend or foe as they smote each other with the sword. Meanwhile, Gideon and his 300 men stood still, with every man in his place, surrounding the enemy camp with the glare of the torches casting an eerie light over the scene as the horns continued to blare (7:21). The Midian host ran in every direction as they cried out in grief and shock, while others fled as fast as they could from the camp. The hostile host fled to Beth Shittah as far as the border of Abel Meholah.

Word went out to Israelites in Naphtali, Asher and all Manasseh to help pursue the Midianites. Gideon also send messengers to intercept those fleeing the battle scene, especially those Midianites attempting to cross the fords of the Jordan to make it home to their native land southeast of the Jordan (7:24). However, two Midianite princes, Oreb and Zeeb ("raven" and "wolf") took temporary shelter in a cavern; one in a rock and the other in the vat of a winepress. They were discovered and slain by Gideon.

By Returning a Soft Answer to Sharp Rebukes – 8:1–3

Gideon knew that speed in his pursuit of the hostile troops was key, for he wanted to overtake these invaders before they could regroup. Now, recall that Gideon came from the tribe of Manasseh, but the brother of Manasseh, the tribe of Ephraim, prided itself on the preeminence that had been given her in the blessing of Jacob and Moses, and on the fact that Joshua had come from their tribe. Manasseh, however, could claim that the tabernacle was located in their territory, and that they had the largest number of people. So a strong sense of envy and natural disaffection was often on Ephraim's lips (Isa. 9:21). Their pique with Gideon was that they had not been called to fight the Midianites. All too frequently in life, too many are not ready to volunteer their services until the real danger is past and then they are ready to censure those who showed zeal and courage in showing up first and they are criticized for the way they handled things. So, the Ephraimites severely chided Gideon with sharp rebukes (8:1).

Gideon responded in a proverbial mode by comparing the grapes of Ephraim as better than those from the vintage of his people in Abiezer of Manasseh (8:2). He offered not one word of recrimination against Ephraim, even though he might have justly said something like: "If God has been pleased to honor me, why should you take offense?" Instead, Gideon wisely held back pushing his victory in the face of the Ephraimites, which he might otherwise have been tempted to do. As Proverbs 15:1 says, "A soft answer turns away wrath" (see also Prov. 16:32; 19:11; 25:15).

This brings out the principle that the only way to appease unreasonable wrath is by adopting a spirit of meekness and forbearance, for once there is a willingness to forego the honor(s) we deserve, it will be a smaller matter to take censure without a cause. Therefore, Gideon praised the Ephraimites for their success, for God had delivered the two princes of Oreb and Zeeb into the hands of the Ephraimites (8:3). This abated their anger as he assumed a lower position of honor than they loudly tooted.

By Answering Fools According to Their Folly – 8:4–35

While the other Israelites likely returned to scoop up the spoils left on the battlefield, Gideon and his brave 300 men pursued the kings of Midian. This small force continued across the Jordan, apparently just north of where the Wadi Jabbok enters the main river. Gideon and his troops followed the wadi all the way up to Succoth for some 50 miles (Succoth means "booths," now identified with Tell Deir `Allah in the Transjordan), in the tribal territory of Gad (Josh. 13:27). But by this time, the Israelite corps of 300 were "exhausted" as they kept up the pursuit of the two royals.

The people of Succoth in Gad, however, were not in a mood to cooperate. Gideon requested, "Give my troops some bread; they are worn out and I am pursuing Zebah and Zalmunna, the kings of Midian," The Gadites clearly looked on this whole affair as a suspicious one doomed to failure by such a small fighting group that was with Gideon (8:4b).

The officials of Succoth rudely replied: "Do you already have the hands (*kap*, "palm") of Zebah and Zalmunna in your grip (*yad*, "hand")? Why should we give bread to your troops?" (8:6) Whether they spoke literally or figuratively about the enemy's hands being already cut off and "in hand" or not, they made clear they weren't going to get in trouble with the Midianites until Gideon had the proof that he had indeed subdued these crop-raiders! Gideon declared that once God gave the kings into his hand, he would return to the city and "tear [their] flesh with desert thorns and biers" (8:7).

Gideon and the valiant 300 pressed on to the city of Peniel (or Penuel; cf. Gen. 32:30–31). There Gideon made the same request as he had made at Succoth. Meanwhile, Zebah and Zalmunna, along with the remaining 15,000 troops left to them, had retreated to a town called Karkor, near the source of the Jabbok River on the frontiers of Gad (8:10). Following the caravan route (literally "the way of those who live in tents"), Gideon caught up unexpectedly with those two fugitives from justice apparently just west of Amman. Zebah and Zalmunna were likely relaxing in their campsite, not expecting Gideon at all. Suddenly Gideon, having taken an unsuspected route, appeared and routed the 15,000 who remained (of 120,000 who had fallen earlier by the sword) from each other. In the panic that overtook them that night of Gideon's raid in the Jezreel Valley, they were totally overtaken.

Gideon captured the two Midianite kings and returned to Succoth after he had fought his final battle with the Midianite forces by the way of the "Pass of Heres," whose location is yet unknown (8:13), to deal with the two renegade cities that had refused any relief to Gideon or his army.

At Succoth, he seized a young boy and demanded he write down the names of the city's 77 officials and elders (8:14). Then Gideon confronted those officials who had spoken so brashly to him about having the palms of Zebah and Zalmunna in his hands before they would give them bread. Then, with switches made of desert thorns and briars, he taught officials and elders a lesson as he "threshed" them soundly (8:16). Some scholars, using 8:7 as a basis, read the Hebrew as *wayarash*, "he beat, thrashed" them instead of the MT text's reading of *wayorash*, "and he caused [them] to know," i.e., "he taught them a lesson." It is not clear which one is meant.

Gideon also made good on his threat (8:9) to those in Peniel by pulling down the defensive tower to which these fellow Israelites would normally resort during an attack on the city. Now that he had visited judgment on those who had refused to help him, he asked the two captives: What kind of men did they kill when they raided those Israelites on Mount Tabor? Stupidly, these dudes said the men they killed looked just like Gideon. Somehow he recognized these men were his brothers, so he demanded his eldest son, Jether, kill the two princes. When the boy declined, Gideon took the sword and killed them himself (8:18–21). Tabor, not far from the Midianite camp, likely sent special raiding parties not only to steal food and animals, but to kill off the population as well.

Gideon's followers felt he had won a specular victory and offered to make him their king. He responded: "I will not rule over you, nor will my son rule over you; the LORD will rule over you" (8:23). However, he made one request: that each man give him a gold earring (for it was the custom of the Ishmaelites/Midianites to wear gold earrings) (8:24). Whether this request was out of character or not cannot be said, for others in the Bible did this to establish memorials. But in Gideon's case it had an unhappy ending. An estimated 40 to 75 pounds of gold was made it into an ephod that Gideon placed in his town of Ophrah, and it later became an object of worship and a snare to the Israelites (8:25–27).

When Gideon died, the people of Israel began worshiping the Baals, and they made Baal-Berith, i.e., the "Baal of the covenant," their god— after all he had done in delivering them from the Midianites. In addition to the 70 sons he bore with his many wives, he had a son by a concubine from Shechem, whom he named Abimelech, meaning, "My father [is] king." Then Gideon died at a good old age, and they buried him in the sepulcher of his father Joash in Ophrah. However, the land had rest and peace for 40 years during the days of Gideon (8:28).

But after Gideon passed away, the nation of Israel strayed into all kinds of Baal worship. But what Israel forgot was how the LORD their God had delivered them from the attacking nations. Nor were they very kind to the house of Jerubbaal and all the goodness he had shown them (8:23–35).

Conclusions

1. God called a man named Gideon to lead a diminished force reduced from an original 32,000 to a mere 300 men to face some 135,000 men from Midian, Amalek, and the children of the East.

2. The Lord had Gideon and his servant Purah sneak near the enemy's camp at night to hear a Midianite tell his dream and his buddy give its interpretation, which promised a victory for Gideon and his 300 if they stood still and watched what God would do to the enemy.

3. The tribe of Ephraim complained to Gideon that they had not been summoned to fight, but Gideon answered them softly and said they had participated at key spots.

4. Succoth and Peniel refused to offer aid to Gideon's 300 battle-weary men as they pursued Zebah and Zalmunna. When the two leaders were finally caught, Gideon returned to Succoth and Peniel to teach them a lesson.

5. Gideon refused the people's offer to be their king, but he did ask for a gold earring from the loot of each Jewish soldier. He made it into an ephod, but the people made it into a false god named Baal-Berit, which caused them to fall into idolatry and to forget God.

Lesson 7

Abimelech, Gideon's Son, Seizes the Throne at Shechem

Judges 9:1–57

The city of Shechem (meaning "shoulder" or "back") rested in the valley between Mount Ebal and Mount Gerizim. This valley was called by some the "navel of the land." The capture of Shechem by Joshua and by Israel is nowhere mentioned in the Bible, yet at a time early in Israel's history, a covenant-renewal ceremony was held on the land between Mount Ebal and Mount Gerizim (Josh. 8:30–35). Therefore, somehow earlier in the history of Israel, Joshua was able to lay claim that site. Nevertheless, Shechem had a most hallowed memory in history.

For example, Shechem was the city Abraham first arrived at on his journey from Haran to the promised land of Canaan. It was also the place where the Lord began to reveal himself to Abraham in that land (Gen. 12:6–7). Later, Jacob had also lived there with his sons, along with the sons of Hamor in Shechem, until Simeon and Levi had killed off the people of Shechem in a wholesale genocide in retaliation for the chief's son raping of their sister Dinah (Gen. 33:18–34:31). So, Israel had quite a connection and a long-ranging history with this city of Shechem.

Later still, we learn, from a Tell el-Amarna letter found in Egypt, that Shechem had fallen into the hands of the Habiru in the fourteenth century B.C.E., a group whose identity has often been somewhat connected with the lives of the Hebrews.[1] In fact, the bones of Joseph, the ruler of Egypt, were given their final resting place in Shechem (Josh. 24:32), even though many of the Shechemites were also called the "men of Hamor" (Judg.

---

1. See the fine article by Clyde E. Billington, "The Israelites Are the `Apiru/Habiru in the Amarna Letters," *Artifax* 39.4 (2023), 16–18.

9:28), and they were men who worshiped the pagan god Baal-Berit. At any rate, Shechem, located at the crossroads of trade in Canaan, is the site for our next narrative in Judges. Our person of interest, Abimelech, was not just another judge of Israel. We will look at him much more closely!

Abimelech Seizes the Throne at Shechem – 9:1–6

Once any of God's people know the steps to ruin and to complete failure, they have an opportunity to avoid that destruction, along with its complete falling into that trap of total ruination, if they repent. Abimelech, along with Israel, started on this path of decline into ruin by forgetting the majesty of God and all he had done for them in delivering them from the Midianite incursions (8:33–35). Israel had unwisely adopted the idol of Baal-Berit as one of their deities. They showed no gratitude for the rescue God had previously given to them from Midian. As a consequence, acting in a way that ignored God's grace and the instruments of that same grace, was equivalent to demeaning both God and his servants!

Judge Gideon, in the days gone by, had married many wives, against the Lord's teaching. A son was born to Gideon by means of his concubine from the city of Shechem. This city may well have been a Canaanite town that was later incorporated into Israel through an alliance between these men of Hamor and the men of Israel!

What provoked a lot of trouble, in this case, was that Abimelech decided to trade on the fact that his mother came from this city, so he told his mother's relatives in Shechem that it might be too much for them to endure having seventy rulers (i.e., Gideon's seventy sons) reigning over them. It just might be much more advantageous for the Shechemites to have only one person, such as a native son like himself, to rule over them (9:2).

The mental picture of such a cacophony of rulers must have scared the people of Shechem into taking very poor action, for Abimelech's plan to get the reigning post of being a ruler over Shechem was working like a charm as the people of that city carried his message all over the town!

Abimelech's half-brothers must have decided his logic was correct: Seventy rulers were too many for one city! So, they gave Abimelech seventy pieces of silver as campaign money, taken from the temple of Baal-Berit. With this logic, that the kingship of one person over them is better than the rule of seventy, along with another observation that a close relative might be better than the rule of an outsider, the ruse was complete. With these campaign slogans, Abimelech was off to a flying start. He used the seventy pieces of silver to hire "reckless adventurers who became his followers" (9:4). Together with Abimelech the men of Shechem slew all but two of Gideon's sons on one stone (9:4–5).

So Abimelech organized these ruthless hirelings, who were actually good-for-nothings, to travel from Shechem for another thirty miles north to Ophrah, Gideon's hometown, to slaughter sixty-eight of his father's sons on one stone. But Jotham, the youngest son of Gideon, did manage to get away by hiding himself from them (9:5b). His name means "Jehovah has shown himself to be perfect/honest" (9:5).

With the death of sixty-eight half-brothers, Abimelech had achieved his goal of being officially proclaimed "king" by the lords of Shechem. Therefore, all the men of Shechem came together, meaning the whole house of Millo,[2] and they began to hold a coronation ceremony to install their native son Abimelech at the "Oak of the Pillar." This site was perhaps by as sacred tree in the area of the sanctuary to Baal-Berit, where a stone or pillar was propped up on an oak tree to represent Baal-Berit, as was the case in several other locations (2 Kgs. 3:10; 10:26–27).

Jotham's Response to Abimelech's Seizure of the Throne – 9:7–21

Abimelech's plan would have worked perfectly except for one small detail: Jotham had escaped the sword that devoured his brothers in Ophrah; this he did by hiding from the executioners. Presumably, the search team stopped to get back to town for the ceremony of the installation of their

---

2. The meaning of this phrase "Millo" is uncertain. Some guess that it meant an earthen platform on which they built a tower, but it does seem to act as another name for "nobility."

native son Abimelech. While this was getting underway, Jotham made his way south toward Shechem. As the lone survivor, he climbed Mount Gerizim to deliver a searching and rhetorical message for those assembled for the ceremony—in the form of a fable (9:7).

Jotham's speech had two main parts: the fable[3] itself (9:8–15), and its interpretation (9:16–20). In so doing, Jotham brought what was equivalent to a lawsuit against the nobility in Shechem in the name of his father Gideon. Mount Gerizim is known today as Jebel et-Tor and is located on the south side of the Nablus valley overshadowing the city of Shechem from the south.

Jotham, now situated atop Mount Gerizim, lifted up his voice (likely interrupting the pageantry of the installation ceremony down in the valley), as he trumpeted forth his words of official proclamation, which began: "Listen to me, citizens of Shechem, so that God may listen to you" (9:8). Whether the Lord would give a favorable response or not depended on whether the Shechemites listened to the Lord! Then followed the fable.

In the fable, there was a deep critique of the whole issue of kingship as it was now being observed. Here is how the fable went. Jotham described how some have in the past rejected such a call to take the governance of a city like Shechem by telling a story about trees, when once upon a time the trees went forth of their own accord to anoint a ruler over them.

The first tree approached by the search committee was an olive tree, to which they offered the title of king (9:8). However, the olive tree would not be deterred from its higher calling, which it stated forthrightly: The olive tree's real purpose and place given to it in the order of creation was to bear olives! The olive tree was quite content with its task; moreover, it knew that if it accepted this invitation to royalty, it would end the very function for which it had been created. So, the olive tree declined the offer of the committee investigating the trees (9:8–9).

---

3. Jotham's fable is one of the finest examples in Scripture. It begins with a brief poetic narrative, teaches a moral lesson involving creatures, plants or inanimate objects that speak or behave like humans.

It was decided that the fig tree should be approached next with the same royal offer, but it too recognized its real purpose in God's created order was to produce figs (9:10–11). Why should it give up its task of providing sweetness for mankind to being reduced to being promoted as a king over the other trees? So, the fig tree likewise turned down the offer.

The committee "branched out" and offered a third tree to fill this royal vacancy; this offer was made to the vine. Much like the other two trees, it stoutly rejected the invitation, for it saw its task of providing wine to cheer both God and men and this it saw as being far superior to any royal job promotion (9:12–13). Thus, all three trees were content and happy with the roles God had assigned them at creation. None of them aspired to the rank of kingship and authority over others. Thus, Jotham posed a serious question for the aristocracy of Shechem: Why were all these other trees so bent on having someone leave what they enjoyed and were made to do by their Creator to assume a job that was not in keeping with God's plan for their lives? By now, the tree search committee must have felt they were "'barking' up the wrong tree." They had to "branch out" further!

In desperation, the trees turned to the bramble ('atad, a species of buckhorn). Jotham's choice of the "bramble" was significant, for nothing of value or worth comes from it—not even the wood is worth anything! It is just a pest and a nuisance to any farmer who must constantly watch for any encroachments of its kind into his fields. Left unchecked, it would overtake the whole field and destroy the land for raising crops of food. Added to that fact was its potential as a real fire hazard, for its low-spreading branches of dry tinder could catch fire easily and spread quickly.

The bramble/thornbush was only too glad to receive this honorific invitation (9:15). The bramble also knew the right lingo, for it flippantly said, "If in truth you really want to anoint me king over all the trees, come and take refuge in my shade" (9:15). But how can anything take cover under a creeping menace or a ground-smothering bramble? Brambles give no shade, and they are incapable of offering any protection to anyone.

Instead, the bramble in this story will turn out to be none other than creepy Abimelech himself. His desire for leadership is one for which he is especially unfit. The bramble fit him well! Apparently, this too is what Abimelech and the city of Shechem deserved.

Jotham proceeded to interpret this fable. He began by appealing to the consciences of the Shechemites (9:16). Had they as a people really acted truthfully and sincerely when they offered Abimelech the kingship? No! He had treated his brothers brutally, by murdering them! His deceased father Gideon had, as it were, "cast his life in front of" the Midianite collusion to save all of them from destruction, but this man Abimelech was showing no appreciation for all he had received from his dad (9:17).

Therefore, Jotham argued that what all of them as Shechemites were doing was nothing less than raising an insurrection against his own father's house on that very day, for in accepting this renegade son of Gideon from the Shechemite concubine, for they were also likewise guilty of the crime of murdering Gideon's sons (9:18).

So, if the men of the city of Shechem had really acted honorably, Jotham left it in the hands of God to determine if that was so. But if they had acted with no truth and no honor in their actions, then let fire come out of Abimelech and let it devour them and the men of Beth-Millo and Abimelech himself as well (9:20–21). Then Jotham fled and ran for his life as he went to "Beer," meaning a "well"), where he hid until he heard that Abimelech had also been killed. God's judgment had come.

The Demise of Abimelech – 9:22–55

After Abimelech "governed" (*sarar*, derived from words for "official, captain," but not from the Hebrew word for "king" or "to rule"). So, he governed Shechem for three years (c. 1151–1149 B.C.E.). Obviously, the men of Shechem refused to dignify his leadership with the verb "rule" or "reign." The truthfulness of Jotham's words quickly came to pass (9:22–23). This happened because "God sent an evil spirit between Abimelech and the men of Shechem" (9:23). This meant that God permitted an evil spirit with rough discord and wicked treachery to break out as jealousies between Abimelech and the people of Shechem developed. This rupture began to produce friction and factions of various sorts, which eventually turned into insurrections, civil unrest and bloodshed. The Shechemites broke the covenant they had made with Abimelech and dropped the yoke they were under according to the agreed-upon covenant!

The "cruelty" perpetrated on the sons of Gideon by Abimelech and those men of Shechem who "aided him" was known by God (9:24). The narrative continued in v. 25 by telling just how the evil spirit of dissension began to produce the expected effects, perhaps during a time when Abimelech was absent for a period. So the men of Shechem organized a conspiracy against the very same man they had hailed and cheered as their native son and as the new governing official just three years ago. Note, however, that God is often pleased to punish the evil persons who have executed evil on others to gain their position with the exact same persons who had contributed to elevating the offender to posts of leadership with the identical rods of affliction that they themselves had gathered![4]

The spirit of anarchy grew in strength in the land as a man named Gaal (meaning "to loath"), son of Ebed, came to Shechem. He had once been a citizen of Shechem. He had with him an armed band of soldiers, so it was sort of natural for him to spot weaknesses in Abimelech's governing. Gaal noticed a political vacuum had begun to develop, for the men of Shechem no longer favored Abimelech, but instead were now favoring Gaal (9:26).

Gaal seems to be more than a former resident, for when he returned, the people of Shechem celebrated his arrival by throwing a wild party for him (9:27). The excitement can be seen in their going out into the fields to gather grapes, which they then crushed by tramping on while lifting their voices in praise, presumably for Gaal and their god. Then the party continued as they crashed into the temple of their god Baal-Berit, and as they ate and drank to their hearts' content. But most significant of all, they agreed on cursing the name of Abimelech (9:27).

Gaal addressed the crowd at the height of this party with a harangue that asked questions like: "Who is Abimelech? Who is Shechem?" Gaal

---

4. This thought is offered by George Bush, *Notes on Judges* (1976), 129.

wanted to raise up Shechemite pride by calling attention to Abimelech's being only partly a Shechemite through his mother's lineage, but his father was Jerubbaal; he was not of the total heritage or descent from the Shechemite people, who were descendants of Hamor.

All this seemed to set the stage for Gaal, though he made one miscalculation: he did not know how loyal Zebul, the officer who had been left in charge of the city, was to Abimelech (9:30). Zebul was Abimelech's "officer" or "lieutenant" (*peqidah*) while Abimelech was absent for a time (9:28, 30). Gaal had played the ethnicity card pretty well, but in a different way than Abimelech had done. Gaal claimed to be fully of the same ethnicity as the people of Shechem, whereas Abimelech was only one-half the same. So Gaal urged they cast off this foreigner's rule.

To counter all this, Zebul secretly sent messengers to Abimelech (he may have been holding court in Ophrah, or even in Arunmah, where he may have been setting up a capital) to inform him that this man Gaal, with his brothers, had arrived and stirred up the people against Abimelech's governing (9:31). Zebul urged Abimelech to come during the night and lie in wait as an ambush in the fields so that at sunrise he could advance against the city, for he would know what else he must then do (9:32–33).

Abimelech accepted this advice, so he got ready for the battle by arriving at night and separating his troops into four companies (9:34). As Gaal came and stood in the entrance to the city's gate, Abimelech rose up from his hiding place in the nearby mountains. When Gaal saw the people, he observed to Zebul, who was also in the gate area leading another coalition, that people were coming down from the mountains. Zebul, stalling for time to set an advantage for Abimelech, denied that what he saw were people; those were only shadows (9:36). But Gaal spoke up to Zebul a second time and declared that those were not shadows but people were coming down "the center of the land" (*tabor ha'arets*, likely "elevated ground"), and a second company was coming from the direction of the "Soothsayer's tree" (*'elon me'onenim*), seemingly a place marked as a spot where some went to get a decision or word from the false gods.

Then Zebul showed his true colors, for he proceeded to chide Gaal, "Where is your big talk now?" "Are you the one who asked, 'Who is Abimelech that we should be subject to him?'" (9:38). Here are the men you mocked so arrogantly, so show your stuff now! So, what was there left for Gaal to do but fight Abimelech. As it happened, this son of Gideon fought Gaal and the citizens of Shechem, and so many were wounded or chased all the way back to the gate of the city that it was a complete rout. Abimelech returned to the city of Arumah, and Zebul drove Gaal and his brothers out of what was left of Shechem (9:41).

The very next day, the people of Shechem, apparently in an effort to resume a normal type of life, went out into the fields again, for Gaal and his gang seemed no longer a factor. When this was reported to Abimelech, the man who had no qualms about murdering his own family, turned on his own people and city as he took his men, divided them once more into three separate companies, and set up an ambush in the fields against his mother's own people (9:42–43). Then he attacked them with each of the three companies coming out of ambush against them.

Seeing that plan had worked in the fields, Abimelech moved next against the city itself, and after fighting all day against the lower part of the city, he captured it all, razed what was left to the ground, then spread salt all over its ground (9:45).

When the citizens saw how desperate their case was for those who remained alive in the city and who had by now fled into the tower of Shechem and the temple of Baal-Berit (likely on the acropolis of the city), they were stunned! Not to be denied complete victory or deterred in his goal, Abimelech took his men up on Mount Zalmon with axes, where first they cut off branches, then imitated what Abimelech was doing by hoisting the branches on their shoulders as all of them finally headed back to Shechem. When they got to the tower, he had the men lay their branches against the stronghold and he set fire to the pile. About one thousand men and women died in this inferno set by their relative!

Abimelech was not finished yet; he went to the neighboring city of Thebes, set up a siege, and captured it. But what happened to Jotham's fable that predicted Abimelech's death if he was that bramble? When the people of Thebes also took refuge in their strong tower, they locked themselves securely inside and climbed out on the roof. Abimelech was going to set this tower on fire the same way he had done in Shechem, for he believed he could "match" what they had done in Shechem. However, as he approached the entrance to the tower, a woman dropped an upper millstone on his head and cracked his skull (9:52–53), which must have left him "divided" in his thinking!

In desperation, Abimelech called for his armor-bearer to draw his sword and kill him, for he did not want to go down in history as being "cracked up" by a woman (9:54). His servant obliged, so Abimelech died and the story came to an end. When the Israelites saw what had happened, they all left for home (9:55).

Epilogue and Conclusion – 9:56–57

The Lord surely repaid Abimelech for the wicked way he had acted toward his deceased father by killing off his brothers. By the same token, God made the men of Shechem pay for their participation in his wickedness. Jotham's curse came to be true for both Gideon and the people of Shechem. The story of Abimelech had ended in total disgrace!

Conclusions

1. Gideon's son, Abimelech, born to him by a concubine from the town of Shechem, along with the men he had hired to kill almost all of the seventy other sons of Gideon as he proudly offered himself as a candidate for the office of ruler in Shechem as their native son.

2. The youngest son of Gideon, Jotham, escaped being murdered. He went on top of Mount Gerizim and gave a fable that indicted Abimelech and the men of Shechem for their act of murder, which is exactly what happened.

3. In the Jotham fable, the trees tried to get one of the olive trees, fig trees, or one of the vines to accept the offer of ruling over them, but all declined since they were content with the tasks the Creator had given to them until the tree search committee approached the bramble-ground-cover, which readily accepted.

4. When Abimelech was temporarily absent from Shechem, a former resident named Gaal returned and turned the city against him. Abimelech, with the help of Zebul, a friend he had been left in charge, overthrew Gaal's insurrection and devastated the city.

5. The life of Abimelech came to a "crushing" end with a split decision on his skull, when he attacked the city of Thebes. This decision was rendered by a woman who had resorted to a tower in Thebes and dropped from the roof of the tower a millstone on Abimelech's head this "cracked up" Abimelech severely.

Lesson 8

The Theology of Peace and War: Governors Tola, Jair and Judge Jephthah
Judges 10:1–12:7

The main narrative has been interrupted just three times to include six additional men who exercised some type of oversight, perhaps as governors rather than judges, as Israel was occupying the land of Canaan: Shamgar (3:31); Tola and Jair (10:1–5); and Ibzan, Elon and Abdon (12:8–15). With the exception of Tola, for whom the text explained that he was one "who rose to save Israel," these six leaders do not otherwise seem to fit the pattern and calling of the other men called "judges" in this book. This is not to lessen their significance or designate them "minor judges" as some try to do, but it does seem there was a difference between these two groups of leaders.

After Abimelech died, a man named Tola, meaning "worm," came from the tribe of Issachar, but he dwelt in Mount Ephraim where he "ruled" (*yashab*) for 23 years; when he died, he was buried in Shamir (10:1–2). Insignificant as he may seem, he came from a family of some note, for he was named after an ancestor who bore the same name. In fact, the name Tola is given to only one other person in the Old Testament, and he was the first of four sons of Issachar (Gen. 46:13; Num. 26:23; 1 Chron. 7:1–2), which shows "Tola" was an authentic name in the tribe of Issachar.

Tola was followed by Jair, who came from Gilead just like Judge Jephthah. Jair ruled (*yishphot*) for 22 years and bore 30 sons, who rode on 30 donkeys, and each son ruled over one of the 30 towns in Gilead, which were still called "Havvoth-Jair," meaning "tent villages of Jair" (10:3–5). Jair's name meant "May [God] enlighten," and one of his descendants gained control over a number of these Transjordanian villages in Gilead

(Num. 32:41; Deut. 3:14). In modern days, Jair would likely be accused of nepotism for installing all 30 of his kids as leaders in each of those towns, but this did not seem to be part of any ancient Near Eastern concerns.

But the scene will turn from a 45-year period of rest and peace as Israel once again goes to serving a whole list of foreign gods and idols (10:6). This will bring up the judgeship of Japhthah as he was finally selected to fight the Ammonites by the inhabitants of Gilead.

God Allows His People to Be Sold Into the Hands of the Ammonites and Philistines – 10:6–18

With the passing of Tola and Jair, and their 45 years of peace, God's people stopped serving and worshiping the Lord, serving instead the gods of Syria, Sidon, Moab, Ammon and Philistia, including all their the Baals and the Ashtaroth (10:6). The people of Israel became theological universalists as they adopted every known god of their neighbors. But they were going to learn, even as we must in our day, that no one can serve the Living God and mammon. Our Lord must have his people's *whole* heart!

For the first time since 3:8, the text mentions God's anger. And for the first time, he will sell his people into the hands of two nations, one to the west, the Philistines (see Judg. 13–16) and one to the east, the Ammonites (see Judg. 11:1–12:7). Scripture takes up the narrative of Jephthah and the Ammonites first and then deals with the Philistine oppression.

The enemy had not become softer or more compassionate in their attacks against Israel. They intensified their fight; for 18 long years they "shattered" and "crushed" the Israelites who lived on the east side of the Jordan, in Gilead (10:8). Ammon also had crossed over to the west side of the Jordan to attack Judah, Benjamin and the house of Ephraim (10:9).

Israel finally came to her senses. With a cry of distress they confessed to God: "We have sinned against you, forsaking our God and serving the Baals" (10:10). But what seemed genuine proved false and untrue about their real worship, for the Lord came back with three separate charges. He was quick to remind Israel of his numerous past favors of delivering them, listing seven nations he had rescued from bondage and rough treatment. Per 10:11–12, these nations were:

1. The Egyptians: their release of Israel under Moses and Aaron (Exod. 12:31–50)
2. The Amorites: Moses' triumph over Sihon of Heshbon and Og of Bashan (Num. 21:21–35)
3. The Ammonites: Ehud's victory over Moab who were allied to the Ammonites (Judg. 3:15–30)
4. The Philistines: Shamgar's victory over them (Judg. 3:31)
5. The Sidonians: Barak's victory over them (Judg. 4)
6. The Amalekites: allies with the Moabites and the Midianites (Judg. 3:13; 6:3, 33; 7:12)
7. The Moanites (perhaps the Midianites as in the LXX): Gideon's victory (Judges 7–8).

The Lord did not take Israel's confession to be real by any stretch of the imagination; they showed treasonous acts all over despite their pious talk (10:13). In fact, if Israel wanted to cry out and entreat someone to help them, God remarked, let them go and cry out to the gods they had opted to worship (10:14). God said: "I will deliver you no more" (10:13b). However, as absolute as this statement sounds, commentator George Bush said it must not be understood as unconditional, for God's threats are always accompanied by mercy to those who truly repent.[1]

The Israelites surprisingly heeded God's discipline. They "put away the strange gods among them and served the LORD. And his soul was grieved for the misery of Israel" (10:16). But a literal translation is "his soul was shortened" (qatsar, "to be short") because of Israel's woes. The Hebrew meaning of the verb expresses that a person is "shortened," "contracted," "straitened" in his state of mind. It is the opposite of being long-suffering or showing forbearance; there is a divine sympathy that can come along with the suffering and with a sort of impatience in responding to it.

---

1. This explanation comes from George Bush, *Notes on Judges* (1976), 140.

As the Ammonites gave their own call to arms in Gilead, the children of Israel also gathered and camped out at Mizpeh (10:17). The foremost question on their minds was, "Who is the man who will take the lead in attacking the Ammonites," for after the fight is over, they promised, that man will be rewarded, for he will be the governing head over all those in Gilead (10:18). They were desperate for any kind of leader, to say the least!

God Knows the Past Treatment of Jephthah's Brother to Him – 11:1–11

Unlike most of the other passages that describe each judge's rise to power, there is no note that says God was the one who called Jephthah for the task of conquering the Ammonites; nothing appears until 11:29, where we are finally told that the Spirit came upon "Jephthah." He is simply introduced as "Jephthah the Gileadite," whose name means "he [the LORD] has opened," and he was "a mighty man of valor" (11:1). But he also was the son of a harlot and a prostitute, so he was conceived in an unlawful situation. Jephthah's wife bore him other sons (11:2), so why did he need a harlot?

When Jephthah's sons grew up, his family threw him out of the house he was born in. They told him in no uncertain terms that he would inherit nothing from his father's house, for he was the son of "another woman" (11:2b). So he fled his brothers and took up residence in the land of Tob, where he began his life of banditry and brigandry by gathering around himself a group of "worthless men," who aided him in being part of the raiding parties who intruded into the towns and villages of Gilead to rob and steal (11:3). Jephthah became one tough guy!

Some time later, the men of Ammon made war with Israel. The capital of Ammon was Rabbah, which had gathered strength and visibility over the years. However, the Israelites living on the eastern bank of the Jordan in Transjordania had grown progressively weaker, and they suddenly realized their need for help if they were to rid themselves of the Ammonite scourge.

No likely candidates were available for such a task of deliverance, so it was time for those who had treated Jephthah harshly by throwing him out of their house to eat crow. The elders of Gilead were sent off to meet with

Jephthah to persuade him to accept this opportunity to be their leader and ruler. They asked him, "Come, be our commander in chief so we can fight the Ammonites" (11:5–6). But these hard-nosed businessmen were very careful not to offer too much. But in their original decision (10:18), they'd promised whoever took this position of the "headship" of these Israelites (*ro'sh*, "head"), would be rewarded. Now they reduced their offer to a "chieftainship" (*qatsin*, "leader, man in authority").

Jephthah may have been disowned by his half-brothers, but he knew he had the advantage in a bargaining situation. So, he countered with his own questions: "Didn't you hate me and drive me from my father's house? Why do you come to me now, when you're in trouble?" (11:7) His point was that these desperate elders could begin their bargaining by reinstating him as a full citizen of Gilead. If they were to get any help from him, they had better come up with a better offer than mere chieftanship, and they were totally out of options! So the elders said in v. 8, "We are turning to you now; come with us and fight the Ammonites, and you will be our head over all who live in Gilead." They were starting to see a fellow human had been wronged, so it was time to apologize and to be reconciled.

Jephthah still had his doubts, so he asked if he would really be their head if he was successful against the Ammonites. They swore an oath: "The LORD is our witness; we will certainly do as you say" (11:10). So Jephthah went with the elders of Gilead and the people made him head and commander over those in Gilead (11:11).

God Knows the Disputes Men Have Over History – 11:12–28

Without wasting too much time, as soon as Jephthah was confirmed as head over the Israelites, he decided not to make war until he had sent messengers to the king of the Ammonites to ask, "What do you have against us that you have attacked our country?" (11:12) To his credit, this "mighty man of valor" did not use this moment as a pretext to show off (to those who had just hired him) his abilities to conduct warfare and gain some of the esteem and honor his family denied him. No, he exhibited prudence and piety as he followed the rules of warfare as taught by Moses

(Deut. 20:10–18). These rules warned that Israel was not to make war with the people and nations of Canaan until they had sent messengers with proposals for peace. Jephthah was not going to have force meet force as his first response; he would wait for the Ammonites to persuade him as to what injustice they had suffered that caused them to take up their swords!

The Ammonite king's[2] response to Jephthah was curt and abrupt. This unnamed king knew Israel had immigrated to Canaan from Egypt, but he was inaccurate in his contention that he and the people of Ammon had been robbed of their territory between the Arnon and Jabbok tributaries (modern Wadi Mugib and Wadi En-Zarqa). The king's statement that the land boundaries between the tributaries were Ammonite land was wishful thinking. True, the territory of Ammon was nebulous and lacked clear geographical boundaries with the desert to the east and the hills of Gilead to the west, but it never included the territory in question. The Arnon had served as the boundary between the Moabites to the north and the Amorites to the south, but it had not included Ammon. Israel had gained possession of the land between the wadis when they defeated the Amorite King Sihon, who ruled in Heshbon over three centuries ago!

Jephthah began by lecturing the king on the historical background of the territories in contention, remarkably drawing on the material in Numbers 20–21 and Deuteronomy 2. Jephthah showed startling historical and biblical knowledge for a man who had been kicked out of his own Jewish family. How much had he assimilated before his abrupt departure?

Jephthah began his reply thus: When Israel came up out of Egypt and knew they had to enter Canaan from the east, which may involve going through Moab and Edom, they treated those lands respectfully. After taking diplomatic steps to get permission to cross Moab and Edom, they were resolutely denied, so they marched around the nations until they arrived east of the Arnon Wadi (11:16–18). Not once did they enter the

---

2. The name and identity of this king of Ammon is unknown, for the name of the first Ammonite king known to us is Nahash (c. 1030-1000 B.C.E.) in 1 Sam. 11:1-2; 12:12; 2 Sam. 10:2.

land belonging to Moab, and not once did the name of Ammon appear in this march. So Ammon had never been robbed of any land!

Jephthah continued that Israel originally had no real interest in any of the land in Transjordania; but since Sihon king of Heshbon, lord over the Amorites, had refused their request to peacefully pass through their land, and answered by gathering his people to fight Israel, the Lord delivered him into Jephthah's hands along with the territory between the Arnon and Jabbok wadis (11:20–21). That is how Israel came to possess the land in dispute! Lastly, Jephthah said, Israel never claimed any land belonging to Edom, Moab or Ammon, only the land that had belonged to the arrogant Amorites (11:22). God had delivered Sihon and the Amorites' land to Israel, so why did the Ammonite king think he should own it? (11:23)

There is a problem with part of Jephthah's speech; he calls Chemosh the god of Ammon (v. 24). This was a god of Moab, not Ammon. Despite Jephthah's remarkable knowledge of Israel's past, he slips up now and again. He does refer in v. 24 to "the LORD our God," but is that proof that he was kosher and completely orthodox in his faith, or did he assert a distinctly syncretistic theology for the purposes of political propaganda?

After having made various points from a historical or theological perspective, Jephthah directed another question to the king of Ammon in v. 25 by asking, in effect, who did he think he was? Did he think he was superior to Balak son of Zippor, the king of Moab? Balak never contested Israel's claim to the land in dispute! Balak never tried to take over that land by coming against Israel to fight for it in battle!

One could also argue, from a chronological point of view in vv. 26–27, that if all along the Ammonites felt the land between the Arnon and Jabbok belonged to them, then why for 300 years had they not acted to reclaim it? Surely, he and the Ammonites knew the Israelites had lived in the contested area for that time. The king's objections on many grounds just did not stand up to the facts. But despite Jephthah's best efforts, the autocrat was not going to listen to him or have his mind changed by any legitimate reasoning; he was downright stubborn and determined to meet Israel on the battlefield. He got his wish!

God Knows the Vows We Have Made to Him – 11:29–40; 12:1–7

When the negotiations between the two men broke off, Jephthah was endowed in an extraordinary way with the Spirit of the LORD. He traveled through Gilead and on across the Jabbok into the territory held by the tribe of Manasseh and then back to his home in Mizpah of Gilead to gather recruits for the upcoming battle (11:29). We don't know how many responded, or what was the attitude of the army he was able to gather, as they went forth.

It seems, however, that Jephthah tarnished his record when he made a rash vow to God in v 30. He seemed to often want to manipulate God by attempting to wrangle concessions and favors from him. But he could also be the opposite sort; in v. 27 he told the Ammonites, "Let the LORD, the Judge, decide." But in this case, he wanted to make a deal with God!

Vows were common during the days of Mosaic legislation and seemed even encouraged by God in difficult times. Jacob, when he had just left his father Isaac and mother Rebekah, vowed that if God would restore him to his home in peace, he would follow the Lord all his days and give him a tenth of everything (Gen. 28:20–22).[3] The Apostle Paul also vowed in Acts 18:18 to bind himself with four others in making a vow. But if a vow was to be acceptable to God, it was to be within the bounds of Scripture. A vow was unacceptable if it involved that which was unlawful.

Jephthah asked in his vow that God deliver the Ammonites into his hands (11:30). But he promised that if God would do this, then "whatever comes out the door of my house to meet me when I return in peace from the sons of Ammon, shall surely be the LORD's, and I will offer it up as a burnt offering" (11:31). What on earth did he think would come to the door—his mother-in law? The family dog?[4] Of course, "to offer a burnt offering"

---

3. Other vows in Scripture include Israel's vow (Num. 21:2); Hannah's vow (1 Sam. 1:11); Absalom's vow (2 Sam. 15:7–8); the Apostle Paul's vow (Acts 18:18).
4. See Walter C. Kaiser, Jr., "[Did] Jephthah Sacrifice His Daughter?" in *Hard Sayings of the Bible* (1996), 193–95.

always referred to an animal offering, not a human! And it was strongly taught in Israel that human sacrifices were an abomination to the Lord.

Anyway, the battle came to an end and the Lord had given to Jephthah a decisive and resounding victory, so the Lord had fulfilled his part of the bargain (11:32). The sons of Ammon were enormously humbled (11:33), for that victory stretched all the way from Aroer up to Minnith with some twenty cities included. The years of Ammonite oppression had come to a sudden end, and surely there was celebration everywhere over the victory.

Meanwhile, Jephthah had moved from Tob in Gilead to his new home and headquarters in Mizpah. And who should come running out to greet him but his daughter, with timbrels and shouts and choruses. Jephthah had no other sons or daughters (11:34)! What was he to do now? Jephthah knew the law forbade human sacrifice. Would the man battle-filled with the Holy Spirit violate God's word in another area of his life? Approval of a person in one area of their life does not equal God's approval of all areas!

Jephthah actually did sacrifice his daughter, tragic as it may seem, going by what seems the most natural reading of the text. He had promised that whoever or whatever comes out of the house "will be the LORD's." Another question arises: Why didn't Jephthah pay the monetary substitute for his daughter (per Lev. 27:1–8)? This would have released her from certain death. Some note that Leviticus 27:28–29 teaches that any person who has been devoted to the Lord may not be ransomed, but the word used for "devoted" in that text is a very technical term (*herem*) used in the conquest of Canaan of devoting a city or its contents (e.g., Jericho) to the Lord. This situation, however, was a voluntary oath and dedication to God.

Thus, there was an annual memorial to her as the "young women of Israel went out for four days [each year] to commemorate the daughter of Jephthah the Gileadite" (11:40). This was not a biblical endorsement of what was done, that event, merely a report of it. In no way are Jephthah's action normative for believers who also make foolish vows to God and feel they must stick to them because Jephthah stuck to his vow!

Jephthah's daughter had told him to keep his vow. "'But grant me this one request,' she said. 'Give me two months to roam the hills and weep with my friends, because I will never marry" (11:37). He agreed, so off she went to do as she said. She had shown enormous filial piety and obedience to her father as she offered to serve the Lord by letting Jephthah fulfill his vow. When she returned after two months, her father "did with her according to his vow; and she knew no man" (11:39).

This section concludes with the Ephraimites once again haughtily complaining to their leader that they had been left out of the summons or troops, in this case by Jephthah, and that they had not been invited to fight the Ammonites (12:1). They had put on this show twice before, once with Joshua and once with Gideon. But as is usually true, the loudest bigmouths and pretenders are also the greatest cowards—and the most at fault when they accuse the innocent. Jephthah reminded them that on the occasion they *were* called, the Gileadites got no help from the Ephraimites (12:2)! Jephthah and his army had put themselves and their very lives at great risk, and the Lord delivered Ammon into Israel's hands, so why was Ephraim now showing up *after* the battle was won? (12:3)

Jephthah rallied the men of Gilead and smote Ephraim mightily. The Gileadites took charge of fords or passages over the Jordan before some escapees from Ephraim got to these crossing points. To tell who was from Ephraim, each person crossing was ordered to pronounce say "Shibboleth" ("stream" or "ear of corn"). Ephraimites would mispronounce it (they could not make the "sh" sound, so they said it as "sibboleth," replacing the Hebrew letter *shin* with *samech*.) The number slain by the army of Gilead was said to be 42,000 Ephraimites, but the Hebrew mode of enumeration is not fully known to us. Therefore, the number may be more like 2040, as the Hebrew copulative *vav* may just stand for "addition." This can be seen from the last census (Num. 26:37), where the entire tribe amounted to just 32,500.

Jephthah ruled for six years, died and was buried in "one of the cities of Gilead" (12:7). The Hebrew uses the plural "the cities of Gilead," but this is an idiomatic usage. Similarly, Genesis 19:29 has Lot dwelling "in the cities" and Jonah 1:5 talks about the "sides of the ship" when only one is meant.

Conclusions

1. The leaders who followed Judge Abimelech were Tola and Jair, under whose leadership Israel enjoyed 45 years of peace and rest.

2. After Tola and Jair died, Israel again indulged in serving and worshiping Baals, Astaroth, and the gods of Syria, Sidon, Moab, Ammon and Philistia, all of which caused the hot anger of God against Israel.

3. The Ammonites oppressed Israel for 18 years until Israel acknowledged their sin in forsaking the Lord. Therefore, God threatened to deliver Israel no more and he told them go cry out to the false gods they had served to deliver them now that they had abandoned him.

4. Gilead had a son named Jephthah, who was a mighty warrior and a person of valor, but since he was the son of a harlot, he was thrown out of his family and cut off from them until a search for a man to lead the Israelites of Gilead against the Ammonites produced his name.

5. Jephthah was called by the elders of Gilead to fight Ammon, which he did with great success. But he failed mightily when he vowed to sacrifice to God whatever came out of his house to greet him when he returned victorious. It was his daughter who emerged to greet him, and he kept his vow, but seriously blemished his record.

Lesson 9

Three Lesser Judges, and Samson Is Born to Manoah and His Wife

Judges 12:8–15; 13:1–25

Three new judges are named as this section turns to what had been going on in the western part of Israel first in the narrative. These three judges seem to have governed during a period of quiet and peace, making it a transitional time between the days of the Ammonite oppression and the Philistine threat that was now occurring on the west side of the Jordan, in the land of Canaan from the Gaza Strip.

The first judge in this interim was Ibzan of Bethlehem, whose name is from a root meaning "swift." He reigned for seven years. He likely wasn't from the Bethlehem in Judah but another one, in western Zebulun, ten miles north of Megiddo (Jos. 19:15). The town in Judah was usually written "Bethlehem-Judah," and the tribe of Judah seems to have been cut off from mingling with the other tribes during this period for some reason.

Ibzan raised a large family, consisting of 30 sons and 30 daughters, at a time when polygamy was widely practiced. Each of the three judges in this period seem quite wealthy, judging by the way they provided donkey mounts for each of their children. Ibzan also arranged for the marriage of each of his daughters to the sons of prominent families.

The second man who judged Israel during this interim was named Elon, meaning "oak, terebinth." He also seems to be from the tribe of Zebulun. He too may have been a polygamist, but the text is silent. He died and was buried in Aijalon ("field of deer") of Zebulun (13:13).

The third and final judge was Abdon ("service"), son of Hillel, a Pirathonite, today equated with modern Far`atah, on the West Bank, some six miles west and southwest of Shechem. Abdon seems to have been the wealthiest of the three judges; his opulence can be seen in the fact that he had 40 sons and 30 grandsons, all of whom rode on 70 white donkeys (cf. 5:10; 10:4). He was judge in Israel for eight years (13:13–15).

Following this period of transition, the text turns to Samson's story.

In His Grace That Is Greater Than Our Sin – 13:1–5

The writer of Judges introduced in 10:7 the dual threat of the simultaneous Ammonite and Philistine oppressions. We should not add the number of years listed as if they were one a continuous series. The author has already covered the Ammonite threat in the east (overlapping with the Philistine challenge in the west) and Jephthah's judgeship. Now the writer takes up the greater concern, the Philistines in western Israel; this covers the rest of the period of the Judges and extends into the opening years of David's reign (2 Sam. 5:17–25). In fact, the Philistine oppression continued until it was finally broken at the Battle of Ebenezer during the days of Samuel, the judge and prophet. So, if Samuel he served for about 18 years when that oppression had begun, it lasted from roughly 1087 to 1047 B.C.E.

These Philistines seemed to have been of Indo-European descent, according to recent studies of some excavated tombs. These Philistines had settled in the Gaza Strip of Canaan somewhere around 1200 B.C.E., even though they may have been using some, or all, of that land previously to produce farm products while they still lived in Caphtor, which may have been on Crete or Cyprus.

At first the Philistines were repelled by Judge Shamgar (3:31), but they still managed to set up their pentapolis in Gaza, Ashkelon, Ashdod, Ekron and Gath in southwestern Canaan. The migration of the tribe of Dan in far northern Canaan did not occur before the days of Samson, but this cannot be determined with certainty, for the tribe was certainly unable to drive the Philistines from the land assigned to them all the days they lived in the coastal zone on the shores of the Mediterranean.

Once more, the old routine of wickedness became reality as Israel "did evil in the eyes of the LORD" (13:1), so it was necessary to use something to awaken Israel to their moral decline and abandonment of worship of God. This time, the Lord used the Philistines for the next 40 years to bring

Israel to their senses. God again had in mind a particular man who would help Israel to begin to be delivered from their oppressors.

The man God used had a father named Manoah, and lived in Zorah. This rather-small town was on the border between Dan (before that tribe moved to the north) and where the tribe of Judah was located, in the Shephelah. These lowlands were about 14 miles west of Jerusalem and 1170 feet above sea level, on the brow of a hill on the northern side of the Sorek Valley. Manoah was from a Danite family, and his unnamed wife was barren. One day, the angel of the LORD appeared to her with a message:

> "Behold, you are barren and childless, but you are going to become pregnant and give birth to a son. Now, see to it that you drink no wine or other fermented drink and that you do not eat anything unclean. You will become pregnant and have a son whose head is never to be touched with a razor because the boy is to be a Nazirite, dedicated to God from the womb. He will begin to deliver Israel from the hands of the Philistines." (13:3–5)

The literal rendering is "Behold, you are barren and bear not" 13:3b). Infertility was common in the days of Scripture; consider Abraham's wife Sarah (Gen. 18:9–15), or Elizabeth, mother of John the Baptist, just to name two. There were three strong conditions, however, put on Manoah's wife: She was not to imbibe in any products of the vine; she was to leave her son's hair uncut as long as the vow lasted; and this son was not to defile himself by touching a dead body! These were the Nazirite vow conditions set out in Numbers 6, Amos 2:11–12 and Acts 21:23*ff.*

Samson, however, was unfaithful. And his mother, while pregnant, was to abstain from anything made from grapes or partake of any strong drinks from fruits, honey or grain. She was also not to touch anything dead. However, we will see Samson violating some of these restrictions.

In His Power Where We Can Add Nothing to That Work – 13:8–16

Once Manoah's wife received this message, she went in search of her husband to relate the visiting angel's word. In her excitement, she didn't ask the angelic messenger his name, or even where he was from. She identified him as a "man of God" (13:6). But she also likely suspected he might be more than just a human being, for she said "his countenance was like the countenance of an Angel of God—very terrible" (13:6b).

Surprisingly, Manoah immediately believed what his wife said. He did not act as Zacharias did at the news that his barren wife would give birth, and became without speech until that baby was born. Manoah had not seen the angel, but his immediate response was one of belief and prayer:

> "Then Manoah prayed to the LORD and said, 'O my Lord, the man of God whom you sent, let him come, I pray, again to us and teach us what we shall do as the boy [is] being born." (13:8)

He showed strong faith in who God was and what he had said. He expressed no doubts about whether God could or would do what he had promised. Manoah did not ask for a sign to verify God's word, as Zacharias did, to believe; Manoah's concern was how they should teach the boy as he grew up! The angel appeared a second time "as she sat in the field," so she "made haste and ran" to her husband: "Behold, the man has appeared unto me, that came unto me the other day" (13:10). Manoah quickly got up and went with his wife to meet this heavenly visitor (v. 11). He asked the man if he was the same one who spoke to his wife before. The angel answered, "I am" (13:11c). Manoah said, "Now let your words come to pass. How shall we order this child, and how shall we do unto him?" (13:12) More literally, he asks what is the right "rule" or "prescription" (*mishpot*)—what kind of training should they give this boy?

The angel's response instead he repeated the instructions he had given to she who would carry this Nazirite child: "She may not eat anything that comes from the vine, neither [was she to] drink wine or strong drink, nor eat any unclean thing" (13:14).

Manoah requested the angel remain long enough for them to prepare him a young goat. The visitor replied, "I will not eat any of your food. But if you prepare a burnt offering, offer it to the LORD." The text adds that Manoah did not understand all that was going on, as he "did not realize that it was the angel of the LORD" (13:16).

Wanting to know more, Manoah asked: "What is your name?" (13:17). He was not inquiring simply after the vocable by which the angel was known; in Scripture, to ask for the name of a person in Scripture is often to inquire about the character and internal nature of the person. But the angel replied: "Why do you ask about my name, seeing it is wonderful?" (*pele'*). This answer made clear God's character as the worker of marvelous and supernatural feats. This is the same one who revealed himself in Exodus 23:20–21, "Behold, I send an angel before you, to keep you in the way and to bring you into the place which I have prepared. Beware of him, and obey his voice, do not provoke him; for he will not pardon your transgressions; for my name is in him." Even more significantly, the name "Wonderful" is one of the names of the Lord in Isaiah 9:6.

In His Majesty and the Dread It Introduces – 13:19–25

Manoah, faithful to his word, took a young goat with a meat offering and sacrificed it upon a rock (as Gideon had done; 6:20–21). Then "the angel did wondrously (*maphlia*); and Manoah and his wife looked on" and (13:19). The text continues: "For it came to pass, when the flame went up toward heaven from off the altar, that the angel of the LORD ascended in the flame of the altar" (v. 20). This was the last time the angel appeared to them, and Manoah realized the man had been the angel of the Lord (v. 21).

Many believed, in those days, that no person could see God and live, and Manoah said to his wife, "We are doomed to die!" (v. 22) But his wife rejoined: "If the LORD was pleased to kill us, he would not have received our burnt offering and a meat offering at our hands, neither would he have showed us all these things, nor would he have told us such things as these" (v. 23). And she soon conceived and bore a son, whom they called Samson, meaning "sun." Some think his name referenced not the celestial body but the shining countenance of the angel of the LORD. Either way, "he grew and the Lord blessed him" (v. 24), showing he was under God's protection.

The Spirit of the Lord began to "move" on Samson's soul (*lepa'am*, from *pa'am*, "anvil," perhaps signifying a hammer's repeated strokes on it) from time to time in the tribal camp of Dan between Zorah and Eshtaol. Moreover, from time to time, Samson showed astonishing examples of valor and strength as evidence God's unique blessing on his life.

Conclusions

1. Following the days of Jephthah's judgeship as he brought relief to the Israelites from the Ammonites reign of terror for some 18 years of oppression on the east side of the Jordan, God was simultaneously bringing relief from the 40 year's that also had begun on a Philistine side of the land with their oppression on the west side of the Jordan.

2. Samson's parents were from the tribe of Dan, who at that time lived in the original land in the southwestern part of Canaan originally given to the tribe of Dan, before they migrated north to the city to Laish with their tribe, later called the city of Dan.

3. Samson's birth was announced to Manoah's wife by an angel of the Lord. Samson would only "begin" to deliver Israel from the Philistines, but it was the Judge Samuel who finally saw the end of the Philistine oppression at the Battle of Ebenezer.

4. Manoah, upon asking the angel of the Lord to give his name, was told it is "Wonderful" or "Miraculous." In giving his name, he was likewise given the character and internal nature of that name, not just the vocable!

5. Samson and his mother were both to vow to God not to eat or drink any products of the vine, touch any dead bodies or eat anything unclean.

6. When it became clear that both husband and wife had met God, Manoah feared they would die. But his wife correctly pointed out if that were so, God would not have accepted their burnt offering nor told them all that he had about the son they would have.

Lesson 10

Samson Takes, Then Loses,
a Philistine Wife From Timnah

Judges 14:1–20; 15:1–20

One day, Samson wandered down the Sorek Valley to the town of Timnah, where he "saw" a woman he greatly liked. When he returned, he told his mother and father he had seen a woman in Timnah, who was a Philistine; she was the woman he wanted, for she really pleased him; so he demanded his parents get this woman for him to marry (14:1–2).

Timnah was a frontier town. It originally belonged to Judah but was later assigned to Dan. It was some 20 miles from Jerusalem and an hour's walk from Zorah. But where was Samson's original home? Judges 13:25 locates him at Mahaneh-Dan, meaning "camp of Dan." Could this mean the Amorites and Philistines had forced the tribe of Dan into a displaced person's camp of tents, for Mahaneh-Dan, since this site was near Kiriath-Jearim, some eight miles northeast of Zorah! We do not know.

Thus, the ongoing story of Samson, whose name appears among the great heroes of the faith in Hebrews 11, also introduces us to one of the most debated characters in Scripture. In particular, his marriage to a Philistine woman raises one of the largest ambiguities gathered around his name. Commentator George Bush best stated the problem:

> The danger of being enticed into idolatry was the reason of the law as it respected alliances with the Canaanites, [but] this reason we cannot [think was] ... equally applicable to connections with the Philistines. Still the law was merely ceremonial, and if God saw fit to dispense with it in regard to any of his servants, he could do so unimpeached. That this was the case in the present instance, there are strong grounds

> from the actual event to believe [so. ...] we do not feel at liberty, from
> the facts recorded, to pronounce a sentence of condemnation on this
> part of Samson's conduct.[1]

True, the law forbade intermarriage in particular with the Canaanites
(Deut. 7:1–5), which the Philistines were not members of that Canaanite
society. But Philistia also had their own idolatrous god named Dagon. So,
the question about Samson being legitimately married to a pagan is
difficult in spite of all the argumentation. But even though Samson's
parents objected to his marrying a Philistine woman, he responded that
"she pleased him well" (14:3). Nor did his parents realize this whole event
"was of the LORD, that *he* sought an occasion against the Philistines" (v. 4).

Others have tried to argue that this was "a visiting husband marriage"
(*sidiqah*), where the husband's work necessitated his being absent for
extended periods of time because of his livelihood, and he would visit his
wife as frequently as his work allowed. But in that case the wife would
live with her father and family. So, let us examine this text more closely to
see if we can isolate some answers to these questions!

By Using the Pleasure of Some to Accomplish a Divine Purpose – 14:1–4

Samson's story is a difficult one in several ways. He was called by
God even before he was born, and then as a young man, the Spirit of God
stirred up his being and empowered him with unusual gifts of strength.
Even though he was gifted with more divine helps than any of his
predecessor judges, he seemed to accomplish less on the corporate level of
the Philistines. On the individual level, he showed up magnificently as one
truly endowed by the Spirit of God, but he did not present any of the
needed qualities of a military leader, nor did he lead Israel in a major
battle against the Philistines.

---

1. George Bush, *Notes on Judges* (1976), 185.

Samson's name is interesting as well, for it contains the Hebrew word for "sun," *shamesh*, with the typical diminutive ending *-on*, meaning "little sun" or "sunny boy." Some try to connect Samson's name with stories about the "strength" in the Greek legend of Heracles, but a better connection can be made from the nearby town of Beth-Shemesh, meaning "house of the sun," a few miles from Zorah and Eshtaol in the Sorek Valley. Perhaps that group of people worshiped and eulogized the sun.

True, Samson was miraculously conceived by a once-barren woman, and he would demonstrate his great strength on several occasions, but the blessing of God seemed to fall more on the parents than on Samson himself. He shows respect to his parents, but he also showed stubbornness and rebellion in rejecting their advice and regarding his Nazarite vow. Samson's life can be viewed in two parts, divided by geography and women: There was the Timnite affair with the first woman (13:25–15:20), and then came the Gazite affair with Delilah (16:1–31). Both parts conclude by noting that Samson's tenure as leader of Israel totaled only the first 20 years of the 40-year-long Philistine oppression (15:20; 16:31). During his years, Samson killed thousands of Philistines, thus fulfilling the promise made by the messenger of God (13:5) that he would *begin to* deliver Israel but would not fully disentangle Israel from the oppressors.

Verse 4b noted the Philistine domination of that area. Archaeological evidence shows a type of "Philistine-ware" pottery during this period, dating to around 1150 B.C.E. This type of pottery was widely scattered throughout Israel in the Shephelah and the Negev. At Timnah, a village on the other side of the Sorek Valley, Samson met his first Philistine love, which surely went against the ban on mixed religious marriages (Exod. 33:16; Deut. 7:3). One imagines how broken-hearted his parents were after they had had such high hopes, given the miraculous circumstances surrounding his birth.

By Using the Strength Supplied by the Holy Spirit as a Sign – 14:5–6

God gave Samson another sign of his agency. Samson was walking to Timnah with his parents to arrange marriage with this girl he spotted some time ago. It seems by now they'd changed their minds about him marrying a Philistine—or was he so resolute in his desire that there was no changing his desire to marry her? So things seemed to have been patched up between parents and son for the present (14:5).

Later, Samson was alone in the vineyards when a lion jumped out of nowhere to attack Samson. Why Samson was in a vineyard is unclear; his Nazirite vow forbade alcohol. Was this a test? Was he being tempted? Anyway, two significant factors appear in v. 6: The Spirit of the LORD "rushed" upon Samson so that he was suddenly infused with such strength that he tore the lion in pieces; but he never told a word of this to his parents. Why did he withhold this? Was this not another work of God that would have comforted their hearts, or had he already planned to use this incident as a riddle at his wedding? Few persons in this world, had they performed such a feat, would hesitate to disclose how God's Spirit had come over them and what had happened. How could Samson hold back so great a story?

By Enclosing a Secret in a Human Puzzle – 14:7–18

Now for the first time, Samson talked with the Timnite girl, and again he liked her very much (14:7). Perhaps on the way home Samson sneaked off to where he had slain the lion; by now the bees had built a hive in the dehydrated carcass. A swarm of honeybees had settled in, likely after other animals had scavenged the carcass, leaving a natural place for a bees to land and build a hive. Samson scraped the honeycomb and took out large chunks of honey, some of which he shared with his parents (v. 8). But he didn't tell them he had taken it from a lion's carcass (v. 9). Here was another violation of his vow—he was not to touch a carcass!

It was on this occasion of his wedding that his parents and a company of friends had gone to Timnah again for the occasion. Samson made a great feast to celebrate (14:10). The word for "feast," *mishteh*, generally refers to a seven-day drinking and eating bout at the home of the bride's parents. Here may be another place where Samson violated his vow. The writer tells us it included a stag party. This was part of the Philistine custom that involved "choice young men" (*bahurim*) from that area; naturally it included drinking to one's heart's content! Did he also drink with these men? We aren't told.

When these young men arrived at the feast and saw Samson (who likely looked a real iron man), they lined up thirty "companions" (an ambiguous term that seems to imply friendly fellows) to accompany him, perhaps as guards. Though these persons were conscripted, or selected from the crowd, they also seemed to be afraid of Samson when they saw his body-build and may have guessed something about his strength.

Samson, however, was not frightened by the presence of these dudes; he mocked the situation and proposed a riddle for. If they couldn't solve it, they'd pay him with 30 suits of clothing (14:12–13). His riddle was short and cryptic, said in six Hebrew words in two parallel lines. No translation seemed needed for these Philistines, who likely understood Hebrew!)…

"From the eater, out came food
And from the strong, out came sweet[s]." (14:14)

Ancient Near Eastern riddles (and Hebrew ones) often used assonance, repetition and semantic ambiguity. This riddle had a dual paradox: one where the eater produced food, the other where a strong person produced sweetness! The men likely thought something in the present situation was being pointed to, but what? The last word, "sweet[s]," seemed to be key, but what could that be, in the context of this wedding? (14:14)

The men worked hard at this puzzle for three days (14:14c), but they were at a loss to solve it. How could they even have a chance? They had not been in the vineyard when the lion attacked Samson, nor were they anywhere to be seen when he visited the vineyard a second time and found a honeycomb in the dehydrated carcass of the lion now full of honey.

Now that the seventh and final day of the feast was arriving, the men were fully aware they couldn't solve this riddle on their own, so they resorted to blackmailing Samson's bride to demand she finagle the answer from her husband, or they would burn her down along with her father's house (14:15). Talk about sore losers! These men meant business!

For the seven days of the feast, Samson's bride cried on his shoulder for him to tell her the meaning of the riddle. No doubt the 30 hinted at what might happen to her and her family, saying something like, "Is your daddy's fire insurance paid up?" As is so often the case, once the riddle was let out to even a trusted friend, it won't remain a secret for long! That is what happened, for once he told his wife the solution, she told it to her people (14:17). So just before the sun went down on the seventh day, and the time was running out to answer the riddle, they came up with the solution: "What is sweeter than honey and what is stronger than a lion" (14:18). Samson had lost the contest, and his companions were smiling again! But not for long!

By Inaugurating God's Purpose God Through the Holy Spirit – 14:19–20

In response to being betrayed, Samson left for Ashkelon, 20 miles southwest of Timnah. This was a major port city of the Philistine Pentapolis. At this very site, to pay for having lost the contest, Samson slaughtered 30 of the town's men and gave their clothes to the men who "solved" it (v. 19). Apparently, Samson was in no mood to go shopping for men's clothing! Disgusted and dejected, he was also in no mood to enjoy a honeymoon, so he went back to Zorah. The honeymoon had gone sour and was off for the time being! Meanwhile, Samson's "wife" was given by his father-in-law to one of the "friends" who had been guarding him (14:20). Wait until Samson finds out about this! This can only mean trouble!

By Using 300 Jackals/Foxes to Torch the Philistine Crops – 15:1–20

Later, at the time of the wheat harvest—which came in Timnah near the end of May or early June, and is associated with the second of the three Israeli festivals, the Feast of Weeks or Pentecost[2]—Samson's anger had cooled enough that he opted to return to Timnah to cohabit with his wife. He took a young goat as a gift for his wife, which must have been the prescribed gift for an offended wife. (That would get her goat!)

Upon his arrival and his attempt to enter his wife's bedroom, his father-in-law prevented him, for he confessed that he had since given the girl to Samson's best man. The embarrassed father-in-law tried to smooth things out by offering Samson her sister, whom he said was prettier anyway. But that did not please Samson: "This time I have a right to get even with the Philistines; I will really harm them" (15:3).

Samson must have stormed out of his father-in-law's house as he went into the fields and caught 300 foxes/jackals. The word used here, *shualim*, can mean either animal, but "jackal" seems preferable in this context Hebrew word is translated "foxes"; a jackal is something between a wolf and a fox. They live in holes in the ground and are prone to live in ruined towns because they provide loads of places to retreat for shelter, and they also prey on dead carcasses. Foxes are more like solitary animals and more difficult to corral, so Samson may have been dealing with jackals and not with foxes in this instance (15:4).

---

2. The other two festivals were: Passover (during the earlier barley harvest) and Feast of Booths or Tabernacles (during the later harvest of figs, grapes, and olives.

Since Philistia was in the grain country, Samson decided to hit them where it hurt. He caught 300 jackals and tied their tails together and set a torch between each pair of tails. He lit the torches and chased them into the fields full of shocks as well as cut and standing grain along with vineyards and olive groves. Just how he commandeered 300 jackals is not known, but surely he found the whole experience "enlightening" (15:5). Perhaps he thought the Philistines might find a "grain" of truth in the whole event! As Samson no doubt paused to watch the fields go up in flames, he must have hummed a little chorus like: "It only takes a torch to get a fire going."

The Philistines wanted to know who ruined their crops and destroyed everything for the whole next year. Not hard to answer; they knew what had happened with the bride's stolen answer to Samson's riddle. The father-in-law had given the girl to another man (15:6). So, the Philistines came and burnt her and her father in their house with fire (15:6c). Recall they had threatened to burn the house down if she didn't get the riddle's answer, and to save herself and her father, she betrayed Samson—and brought on herself the very doom she hoped to avoid. We can't escape suffering by sinning. That is a sure way to bring it upon ourselves!

Samson wasn't done with the Philistines yet. He denounced them, saying if they thought this was the end of it all and he'd be appeased, they were wrong! Samson viewed his wife and family as the objects of revenge, not as subjects of righteousness or justice. So he smote the Philistines "hip on thigh" with a great slaughter (15:8). Then he went down to dwell in a cleft or a fissure of the rock Etsam—a sort of natural fortress!

The Philistines did not take kindly to these attacks; they came in force into Judah and pitched their tents in Lehi (15:9). Lehi is named here no doubt in anticipation of the name to be later given to the slaughter that was to take place with a *lehi*, "jawbone."

The men of Judah reached Samson to bind him and hand him over to their enemy (15:10), as they didn't want any trouble from their overlords, the Philistines. Samson made the Israelites promise that they would not turn on him personally, but they would simply hand him over to the Philistines, which they did, after they had bound him with two new cords and brought him out from the crevice or the fissure in the rock (15:11–13).

But when the Israelites brought him to the Philistines, the Spirit of the LORD came over him in a mighty way so he was able to snap the cords like flax burned by fire (15:14). Finding the fresh jawbone of a donkey, he took it and slaughtered 1000 men in total (v. 15). Employing what's called paronomasia, or a pun using similar-sounding words, he declared, "With the jaw-bone of the ass I have heaped up a heap [of bodies]" (15:16a). In Hebrew: *Bilehiy ha-hamor hamor hamortayim*. Was this a proud boast or an exclamation of grateful and adoring wonderment to the LORD who had enabled him to accomplish so great a victory over so large an enemy?

As he finished speaking, he threw the jaw-bone away and named the place Ramath-Lehi, meaning "The hill of the jawbone." Very thirsty, he called out to the Lord: "You have given your servant this great victory. Must I now fall into the hands of uncircumcised?" (15:18) So God opened up the hollow place in Ramath-Lehi and water came out. Samson drank the water and his strength returned, and so the spring was called *En Haqqore*. Samson judged the Philistines in his days for 20 years (15:20).

Conclusions

1. Samson went down the Sorek Valley where he saw a Philistine woman he loved and wanted to marry. Even though his parents tried to dissuade him, they did not discern that this was of the Lord, apparently was in return for what the Philistines had done to Israel.

2. Samson had the God-given gift of strength. He slaughtered a lion, and he later found the honeybees had formed a honeycomb in its remains.

3. Samson posed a riddle for those designated as his 30 companions. It was to be solved by them within the seven days of the wedding festival or they had to give Samson 30 sets of clothing. If they solved the riddle, then he owed them the 30 sets of men's clothing.

4. The 30 companions finally got Samson's bride to get Samson to tell the solution to the riddle on the last day of the festival, so they won the contest. So, Samson went to the Philistine city of Ashkelon, where he struck down the men of that city, so he could in quick fashion get the 30 sets of clothes he owed as a wager.

5. When Samson's wrath had cooled, he went back to Timnah to be with his bride, only to learn that his wife had been married to his best man. For this insult, Samson went out in the fields of the Philistines and caught 300 jackals, where he tied the tails of every two jackals together, set a torch between the tied tails, and then chased them into the ripe wheat fields, vineyards and olive groves.

6. When the Israelites delivered a bound Samson to the Philistines, because they were Israel's overlords, Samson broke the new binding cords, took a jawbone and he killed some 1000 Philistines.

Lesson 11

Samson's Affairs With the Prostitute in Gaza and Delilah in the Sorek Valley

Judges 16:1–31

Samson decided to walk down to Gaza (modern Ghazzeh), the southernmost city of the Philistine Pentapolis and the most important of the five cities of the people who had moved into that territory around 1200 B.C.E. This city was some 60 miles southwest of Jerusalem, 15 miles south of Ashkelon and about two and a half miles inland from the Mediterranean. Gaza stood on a hill about 2.5 miles in circumference.

His problems with loving and choosing Philistine women continued, for in Gaza he saw a prostitute he loved, so he went to spend a night with her (16:1). Was this prompted by his search for finding another occasion to relieve the oppression of the Philistines, or was it born of pure sinful lust?

Samson Visits a Prostitute in Gaza – 16:1–3

Surprisingly, the narrator never mentions the name of the Lord, not even in Samson's mighty feat of picking up Gaza's city gate and taking it to the top of a hill facing Hebron. Nor does the writer identify the woman Samson had sex with, just as the woman at Timnah remained unnamed. The writer gives us the barest details about this woman in the first three verses and makes no comments on anything from a moral or biblical point of view.

No sooner had he arrived than the word spread: "Samson is here!" (16:1). When he saw this prostitute, Samson went and spent the night with her. But the citizens took immediate action, for the stories of his

JUDGES When Times of Peace and Judgment Reigned

strength likely preceded him. The people formed a military force that surrounded the house where he was with this prostitute and waited for him all night. They planned to lie low until dawn came, then capture and kill him! (16:2)

But around midnight, Samson got up and left. Upon finding that city had been locked down for the night, with the gates shut, with his strength he picked up the two gate's doors and doorposts, and he tore them loose. Then he put it all on his shoulders and carried it to the top of the hill that faced the city of Hebron (16:3). No longer was Gaza a gated community!

Samson Falls in Love With Delilah in the Sorek Valley – 16:4–22

The longest story in the Samson cycle begins almost nonchalantly with what we've by now come to expect: "He loved a woman in the Sorek Valley" (16:4). There's nothing inherently wrong with a man loving a woman, but the problem was the *type* of women Samson chose. Delilah's name comes from the Arabic *dalla* or *dallatum* ("to flirt," "flirtatious"), but Samson may have punnily named her from *d + lyth*, "of the night." The Sorek Valley was a wadi that ran through the northern part of Philistia, from the hill country of Judah and Dan, down to the Mediterranean coast.

When the Philistines heard Samson had arrived, they knew they had to act to capture him. But how? The five lords of the Philistines got together and plotted. They'd get Delilah to coax the secret of his strength from him, like the woman from Timnah had persuaded him to tell the answer to the riddle he'd posed. But the men added one more wrinkle: Whereas the Philistines of Timnah had urged their woman to blackmail Samson by telling her he did not love her and that she and her family would be burned alive, the men of Gaza gave her an incentive: 5500 shekels of silver, 1100 from each of the lords. It is impossible to set the value of the shekels into today's currency, but Abraham paid 400 shekels of silver for the field with the burial plot of the Cave of Macpelah upon the death of his wife Sarah (Gen. 24:15, 19), and the price for a slave was 30 shekels of silver (Exod. 21:32). She'd be set for a good while to come with that kind of money!

Delilah accepted the challenge and began to ply Samson for the solution or secret to his strength (16:6). Samson lied to her and said, "If they bind me with seven fresh animal tendons that have not been dried, then I will become weak and be like any other man" (16:7). The Philistine lords gave her with the tendons and hid in her room. But when she yelled out: "Samson, the Philistines are upon you," Samson snapped those thongs as if they were pieces of string that had come too close to the fire! (16:9)

Delilah scolded Samson for lying and tricking her, for he had plainly duped her with the story about seven fresh thongs (16:10). So, as she tried again to squeeze the truth out of him, he said he had to be bound fast with new ropes (16:11). This enormously strong man did not see through her schemes and realize that somebody wanted him bound up. Again she sounded the alarm that the Philistines were upon him, but he broke the cords like thread. You'd think he would start to realize something was going on!

We can only imagine how distressed and upset Delilah was after being fooled twice. The Hebrew text may be damaged in 16:13–14, but it is restored on the basis of the Septuagintal reading, at least in part; it contains enough correction for us to see how mischievous and ridiculous Samson could be. He told Delilah that if she took and wove his seven locks and fasten them with a pin, he would become weak (16:13–14a). What a load of baloney he handed her! This iron man certainly was not as wise as he ought be! He was playing with fire!

For one more test, Delilah had Samson kneel down and place his head on her lap as she took his seven locks and wove them as if one would weave strands of cloth on a loom. She tightened them with a pin. Samson had fallen asleep; when she said the Philistines had come, he woke, pulled out the pin, and Delilah's so-called discovery was a flop.

She again pulled the old speech that Samson didn't love her, as he had mocked her now three times (16:15). She adopted the blackmail route totally, accusing Samson of not loving her at all. Actually, he had let her get closer to the truth than she knew, for he had told her part of the "hairy details" about his strength. She kept complaining day after day until she vexed Samson's soul so much that he gave to get some rest from her constant bellyaching about his not loving her anymore (16:16).

He couldn't stand the nagging any longer, so he told her the whole story. His will and resolve to maintain the secret of his strength was finally broken. Sensing she had won and that he had finally told her everything as he bared his soul to her, she once more called for the five lords over the Philistine cities to come and hide in her place! (16:17).

For the first time Samson gave away the secret of his strength: "I have been a Nazirite unto God from my mother's womb." If *my hair is shaven* off my head, my strength will disappear from me and I will become weak and like any other man" (16:17). Delilah knew Samson had told her the truth, so when she called for the Philistines to come and hide in her house as she tried one more test to determine his strength, there was an air that she had won (16:18). Once more these five rulers brought their money, for Delilah had told them Samson had told her all that was in his heart (16:18b).

Again she made him rest on his knees with his head in her lap. Then she called a man and said to shave Samson's seven locks. When she yelled that the Philistines were there, Samson at first did not realize his strength had indeed left him. He thought that as before, he'd instantly be back to his former self. But this time was different. The Philistines came out of hiding and captured Samson. They poked out his eyes and carried him off to Gaza, sightless and bound with shackles (16:21). Samson did not realize God had turned from him and he was on his own weak power.

Why the Philistines took Samson all the way to their southernmost city, we can only guess. Were they afraid the Israelites might try to steal him, so they kept him as far away as possible? Maybe the Philistine lords wanted to repay Gaza for the humiliation they had suffered. We do not know. But as time went on, Samson's hair began to regrow after he had been so unceremoniously shaven (16:22). The Philistines stupidly missed this, but it set things up for the final act in Samson's unique career.

Samson Pulls the Palace Down on the Philistine Rulers and Their People – 16:23–31

Overjoyed, the Philistines celebrated their triumph. This festival they dedicated to their god Dagon, named from *dag*, "fish." At the site of Ugarit, Syria, which was destroyed by the Philistines, Dagon is named as the father of Baal by his title *bn dgn*, "son of Dagon." The Philistines chanted:

> "Our god [Dagon] has delivered our enemy into our hands,
> The one who laid waste of our land and multiplied our slain." (16:24)

At the time when their merriment and joy was at its peak and they no doubt were by then full of wine and truly in their cups, they brought Samson out of his prison house to mock him and to make as much fun as they could of his wretched newly achieved weakness (16:25). They made him the laughing-stock of the country as they hurled insults at him. But as the Puritan commentator Matthew Henry commented, it surely was true that:

> "Nothing fills the measure of the iniquity of any person, or people, faster than mocking, or misusing the servants of God, yea, though it is by their own folly that they are brought low. Those know not what they do, nor whom they affront, that makes sport with a good man."

Foolishly, the Philistines allowed Samson to be stationed at the festival between the two pillars that supported the upper or half-story or loft on the second floor as well as the roof of the building (16:25c). The reader can guess by now what would happen—the structure came crashing down!

No temple to Dagon has yet been found at Gaza; but a building in Stratum X uncovered in Tell Qasile by archaeologists[1] is a good match for the building Samson had employed for his great "letdown" of the Philistines.

In a pathetic picture, specifically vv. 26–27, our sometimes-hero Samson asked the "young man" (na'ar) in charge of him to let him lean against the pillars that supported the temple. Samson had a plan: He would make a grand exit from this earth and from the tasks God had helped him to accomplish. We are told in v. 27 that all five Philistine lords were at this festival, as were the people of Philistia—adding up to some 3000 men and women who engaged with delight in making sport of Samson.

In one last mighty cry out, Samson called on the Lord:

> "O Sovereign LORD, remember me, O God, please strengthen me just once more, and let me with one blow get [my] revenge on the Philistines for my two eyes." (16:28)

With that call to God came the mighty collapse of the building along with Samson's death. It's unclear if this also took the lives of the five lords, but 3000 lives were lost for certain, for the two pillars that Samson had pulled down supported the upper floor that was also packed with Philistines.

Samson's family no doubt heard of the tragedy in Gaza, and that he had died in the midst of it, so his brother's and all his father's family went down to Gaza to gather his remains so they could bring him back to their place between Zorah and Eshtaol and bury him in the tomb of his father Manoah.

---

1. A. Mazar, "A Philistine Temple at Tell Qasile," in *Archaeology of the Land of the Bible*, 319–23.

Conclusions

1. Samson went down the Sorek Valley to visit the capital of five lords of the Philistines in Gaza, when he saw a harlot, with whom he decided to spend the night making love.

2. When the excited citizens of Gaza heard that Samson had come, they surrounded the harlot's house all night, expecting to capture him in the morning. But he got up and left at midnight, carting off the double doors of the city gate that had been locked to keep him there. These gates he carried to the top of the hill that faced Hebron!

3. Later, Samson fell in love with another women in the Valley of Sorek named Delilah. The five rulers of the Philistines offered to pay Delilah 5500 shekels of silver (1100 from each ruler) if she could extract from Samson the secret of his strength. She accepted this challenge.

4. She coaxed Samson four times, arguing he did not love her unless he reveled the secret of his strength to her. She kept nagging until he finally told her he was a Nazarite from his birth and if his hair were cut off, he would be weak as other men. She hired a man to give him a quick trim and haircut, resulting in his career being "cut short"!

5. The Philistines captured the shaved Samson, poked out his eyes and left him to grind grain for them until a feast day came along when he was brought out for public ridicule and mocking. Led by a servant, he asked the boy to help him over to the two central pillars supporting the temple. Asking God for one last burst of strength, Samson pulled the whole building down, possibly on the five Philistine rulers, along with 3000 people of Philistia who likewise died with him in a crashing decrescendo.

Lesson 12

Micah Steals From His Mother and Installs a Levite as His Priest
Judges 17:1–13; 18:1–31

Judges' third major section, often called the "Appendix," is chapters 17–21,[1] which can be divided into two parts: 17:1–18:31, the tribe of Dan moves north to the city of Laish with a Levite hired as their priest; and 19:1–21:25, the near-eradication of the tribe of Benjamin because of the sin that took place in Gibeah. Interestingly, both tribes, Dan and Benjamin, had originally been assigned territory right in Israel's heartland, between the tribes of Judah and the two from Joseph. Perhaps the author of Judges was guided by the Holy Spirit to choose the stories from these tribes, which were by no means living on the fringe or in the distant territories of Israel, to show how evil and sin itself had infiltrated the very heartland. The sins of Israel were not just at the fringes of Israelite society, but they were at its very center!

This section's repeated refrain is how far the nation had drifted from God. "Everyone did as he saw fit" (17:6; 21:25) because "In those days Israel had no king" (17:6; 18:1; 19:1; 21:25). Both sections feature stories of Levites, whose priestly character was very different from what one might expect. Israel not only fell into idolatry of making and worshiping homemade shrines of multiple gods, but also for making their own *ephod* and *teraphim*; they also chose and installed their own priests as they thought best. Israel and her culture were by now definitely falling away from the God who loved them and had called them to be a blessing to the whole earth.

---

1. The three parts of Judges: (1) Prologue, 1:1–2:5; (2) the book of the Deliverers, 2:6–16:31; (3) Appendix, 17:1–21:25.

When We Have a Disconnect Between Right and Wrong – 17:1–6

A Cursed Son

The Appendix begins with the phrase *wayehi 'ish*, "Now there was a man." This apparently was an ordinary man the writer chose from an unremarkable family who lived in the "hill country of Ephraim." Fascinatingly, the character in this story is named Micah (from *mikayehu*, "Who is like God?"). This name appears 18 times in 17:5–18:31!

Micah's mother had cursed the person who stole her eleven hundred shekels of silver. Micah, overhearing this, immediately confessed that he was that thief (17:2). His mother tried to reverse the effects of her curse by adding: "The LORD bless you, my son!"

A Cursed House

But from that point on, matters turned even more sour and contrary to the word of the Lord, for she then said, "I solemnly consecrate my silver to the LORD, for my son to make an image overlaid with silver" (17:3). She gave him 200 shekels to use to make an idol. What on earth is going on here? God had long ago provided a means for proper restitution of stolen goods (Lev. 6:1–7), but that was not the way Micah and his mother chose. A person was to add 20% to what they had stolen to satisfy the concerns of the robbed, plus additional for trespass. But this Levite agreed with his mother to image of a pagan god made! That is precisely what the law forbade in Deuteronomy 27, along with twelve other curses. Verse 15: "Cursed is the man who makes a *pesel* ['carved image'] or a *massekah* ['molten image']." Often a person or nation could have all the trappings and paraphernalia of worship and yet be under God's judgment, because these false substitutes were not at all a proper offering to the One whose majesty, holiness and whose person as the Living God exceeded all else.

"Everyone did as they saw fit"; Micah exemplified this. Even their worship of the Lord of the universe was a matter of their own devising! The writer of this episode with Micah literally contrasted his "house of God" (17:5, often rendered "household gods") with the true "house of God" at Shiloh (18:31). Micah also installed one of his sons as his personal priest in his house as he tried to manipulate God and set up his own rules for worship, thinking he would be blessed. But homemade religion is no religion at all! And his mother thought she was making a gift to God, at first consecrating the total shekels to the Lord, then gave part of it to idolatry. How foolish!

When We Have a Disconnect Between True Ministry and False Ministry – 17:7–13

A Minister for Hire

The focus shifts to the sudden appearance of an unemployed seminary student (actually a Levite) from Bethlehem, one of the 48 cities allotted for the Levites to live (Num. 35:1; Josh. 21:1). He had been living in the clan of Judah (17:7) but traveled north to seek employment elsewhere, and he came upon Micah's house in the hill country of Ephraim (17:8).

An Unemployed Minister Is Now Employed

Micah asked him, "Where are you from?"

"I'm a Levite from Bethlehem in Judah," he said, "and I'm looking for a place to stay." (17:9)

Then Micah urged him: "Live with me and be my father and priest, and I will give you ten shekels of silver a year, your clothes and your food" (17:10). The Levite thought that a pretty good offer, for it included room, board and a provision for the professional outfits he would wear. He became like one of his sons. But later this man turned out to be available to the highest bidder (cf. 18:19–20). Micah, his prospective employer, evidently concluded that if it looks like a minister, talks like a minister and acts like a minister, then it must be a minister! Micah believed God would now bless him because he had a real live minister in his own house performing religious services. It is a huge mistake, however, to think that what passes for true worship and consecrated ministry is so. Worship of the Living God is not an assembly of worship items, like several teraphim, a collection home-made-idols, robes and invented liturgies.

When We Have a Disconnect Between True Worship and False Worship – 18:1–31

A Lawless Disrespect for the Property of Others

Joshua had originally assigned the territory that the tribe of Danites were to occupy by dislodging the Amorites from the coastal spot they inhabited, for in this way, the Danites could have as their own, a territory that was just west of the tribe of Benjamin and east of the Mediterranean Sea (Josh. 19:40–48). However, the tribe of Dan never succeeded in accomplishing that command from Joshua, therefore they were pressed into a small bit of geography, apparently between the cities of Zorah and Eshtaol.

Therefore, the tribe of Dan decided to send out five men of valor (*gibbor he-hayil*, "men of strength" or "mighty men of valor") from the Danite towns of Zorah and Eshtaol to spy out any possible land where the people of Dan might migrate to live instead of the unconquerable quarters Joshua had assigned them. They were to seek out living space for the tribe, for they were too crowded and some of the territory they felt they could not conquer. This did not mean the whole tribe of Dan moved; Samson's family did not move with them when later on, in a partial exodus, some went north to Dan.

The five scouts Dan sent out were to spy: "Go, explore the land" (18:2). When they arrived at Micah's house, while they were on their search, the young Levitical priest greeted them. Apparently Micah wasn't home, but they recognized the young Levite's voice (18:3). The Danites were recognized perhaps by their accent, so they asked him who or what had brought him there. The Levite proudly answered: "[Micah] has hired me and I am his priest" (18:4). The scouts requested, "Inquire of God, please, that we may know whether our way on which we are going will be successful." The priest replied, "Go in peace; your way in which you are going [a]has the Lord's approval" (18:5–6). Did God actually communicate that message to this compromised Levite, or was he merely attempting to say what he thought was the message they expected? Scripture does not directly say it was revealed by God, so the question remains.

The five men left Micah's house after staying one night and later they came to Laish, the city in the far north (also called Leshem; Josh. 19:47; Dan. 5:29). The inhabitants of this city seemed to have been a colony mostly of Sidonians, or people who adopted their lifestyle. The scouts give us only two ambiguous words to describe these people: *betach* and *shoqet*. The first is from the root for "to trust" and thus could mean either a people who were "confident" or "carefree," "careless" and "unsuspecting," while the second word came from the root "to rest" and could mean either the people of Laish were "peaceful" and "tranquil" or "relaxed, idle." Did the writer mean both opposites were true of these inhabitants? (18:7)

But why did the people living in Laish feel secure? It seems because there were no adversaries around to trouble them. Moreover, the land had an abundant water supply that flowed constantly from the melting snow flowing down off Mount Hermon, so in this regard, the people lacked nothing and were prosperous (18:7b). And since they were separated from Phoenicia's city of Sidon where many of their relatives lived by the high Lebanon Mountains, the coastal Sidonians must not have taken any interest in their relatives in the remote inland town of Laish, for the Sidonians were otherwise totally caught up in a burgeoning maritime trade. The Laishites also had no overlords or restraints, acting as a free republic. No opposition came their way from the other nations that frequently challenged one another.

The five scouts returned to the original Danite cities of Zorah and Eshtaol to report what they had found in this city of Dan (18:8). These spies were most enthusiastic about the site of Laish, for they wanted the tribe to move immediately north (18:9). The land, they assured, "It is very good." Their praise was unbounded, for the land was both good and beautiful. More, the people were completely unsuspecting of any intruders or opponents, thus there was plenty room for everyone, and the land seemed to possess no deficiency, for it was most resourceful in every way (18:9–10). The scouts concluded their praise of the land with the pious note that "the LORD has given [this land] into our hands" (18:10).

We are not told how many of the Danites responded in agreement with the challenge to pick up immediately and move to the far north, but we read that only 600 of their men armed for battle set off from Zorah and Eshtaol when the time for a move came (18:11). This number seems very small; in an earlier text, Deborah and Barak had led 10,000 men from other tribes such as Zebulun and Naphtali against Captain Sisera (4:14).

The first stop of the transitioning caravan made on the first day was at Kiriath-Jearim, eight or nine miles from their home base of Zorah and Eshtaol, one of the four towns of the Gibeonite confederacy that had entered into the Israelite alliance by their act of duplicity and lying against Joshua and his men about their identity and homeland (Josh. 9:17). There they halted at a campsite called Mahaneh-Dan, meaning the "encampment of Dan," which was "behind," i.e., to the west of Kiriath-Jearim (18:12).[2]

This Danite migration moved on the next day to the hill country of Ephraim near the home of Micah, where the spies had stayed for one night during their scouting mission (18:13). When they got to there, the 600 Danites, who were armed for battle, stood at the gate as the five scouts went inside to take the carved image, the ephod, the teraphim, any other household gods, and the cast idol that would be used in their own future times of worship in the area to which they were traveling (18:17)!

The priestly Levite asked, as he saw the scouts: "What are you doing?" That deserved the prize for best question of the day, for it was quite obvious! The Danites did not bother to answer except to say:

---

2. In the world of the ancient Near East, the face is always to be toward the east, so what is said to be "behind" one is the west just as Deut. 11:24 designates the Mediterranean Sea as the sea behind them, and the east is what is before or in front of others who are pointing east.

"Be quiet! [Or: 'Shut up!'] Don't say a word. Come with us and be our
father and priest. Isn't it better that you serve a [whole] tribe and clan in
Israel as priest rather than just one man's household?" (18:19)

Naturally, with 600 armed men stationed at the gate, it all was a most
persuasive form of argumentation, for the Levite was completely stifled
(even if he had wanted to make such an objection from making any kind
of a protest as he stood by helplessly as all the idols and worship items
were being taken. We can hardly miss the extent of spiritual degeneracy
that Israel experienced as the writer repeated the list of Micah's pagan
religious paraphernalia ("ephod, teraphim, graven image, and molten
image"; vv. 14, 17, 18, 20). It was an abominable list to say the least!

The young Levite was moved by the military-backed-logic of the men
from making any argument. Anyway, he would indeed have a much larger
group of people to minister to rather than just one man and his household,
so he rejoiced in his good fortune to have a chance to serve a larger
congregation. He voluntarily took charge of Micah's religious
paraphernalia and went with the Danites as he took his place in the middle
of their entourage. As the contingency left from Beth-Micah, i.e., Micah's
makeshift temple, they must have expected trouble would sooner or later
come when Micah learned what they had done, so they arranged their
touring group so the children, livestock and possessions were in front of
the entourage (18:21).

The men of Dan were not disappointed in their suspicions, for after the
whole group had gone some distance, Micah saw the theft. He caught up
with these thieving migrants. The Danites, acting surprised by this turn of
events, yelled back to Micah and his reinforcements, "What's the matter
with you that you called out your men to fight [us]?" (18:23). The verb the
insolent robbers had used for "called out" was za'aq, "to summon a
militia" or "a battle cry." This same verb has been used for the previous
cries of Israel to God about the oppression of foreign enemies (6:9–10;
10:10-14); however, this time the oppressors who were sent by the Lord

were fellow deviant Israelites who were about to teach another part of the nation of Israel a lesson for stealing Micah's shameful gods.

A Lawless Substitution of False Worship for True Worship of God

In lawless disrespect for others' property, unorthodox as it was, Micah was left complaining that the Danites had taken "the gods I made and my priest" (18:24). Now there's a theology filled with irony, if there ever was one! Note the repeated use of the verb *laqah*, "to take" (18:17, 18, 20, 24, 27). He literally pleads, "What to me still?"—i.e., "What's left for me [now that you've betrayed and robbed me]?" He felt the forces of evil had left him in despair! Thus, Beth-Micah, which had its origins in a double theft, is now left with nowhere to go but back to his house. Can a divine blessing come to such a thieving and idolatrous people? Everyone is doing whatever they think according to their own measure of right and wrong!

The Danites assume a rather cool, but detached sort of attitude as they boldly warned Micah and his vigilante group:

> "Don't argue with us [or: 'shut up'], or some hot-tempered men will
> attack you and your family will lose your lives." (18:25)

Micah saw the 600 men clearly outnumbered him, so he turned and went home now stripped of his gods and worship aids (18:26. But the men of Dan continued on their way to Laish. When they got there, they attacked the unsuspecting city with the sword and burnt it down (18:27), for there was no one nearby to rescue them; they lived far from Sidon in the Valley of Rehob, and they had no relationship with anyone else, so they were defenseless and had no any helpers to assist them (18:28).

The attacking Israelites rebuilt the city and named it Dan, the name of their father (18:29; cf. Josh. 19:47). Worse still, the men and women of Dan set up for themselves idols. The Levitical man, whom we have seen as the young priest in this story, is now identified as "Jonathan, the son of Gershom, son of Moses;" he and his sons now served as priests as a sanctuary was set up in Dan until the captivity of the land (18:30). Look what the line of Moses had become! They also continued to use Micah's idols, even for as long as the Tabernacle of God was in Shiloh (18:31).

That this Levite came from the line of Moses so embarrassed many of this Scripture that some Hebrew texts tried to save face by changing "son of Moses" to "son of Manasseh." To do this, the Hebrew consonants for Moses (*Msh*) often had a supralinear *nun*, standing for the letter **n** after the first Hebrew letter *M* for *MSH* in Moses' name, changing the Hebrew from "Moses" to "Manasseh" (see Exod. 2:21–22). But almost every commentator says the original text read "Moses," so it should be read that way, even if it is shameful that one of Moses' sons was involved in idolatry.

Later, the Israelite site of Dan would be one of the two northern sanctuaries where Jeroboam I would install one of the two golden calves or bulls. That spot is still visible to day at the archaeological site of Dan.

Conclusions

1. This chapter began with Micah's mother cursing whoever stole her silver. When Micah overheard, he quickly confessed he was the culprit.

2. Micah's mother tried to reverse the effect of the curse by asking God to bless her son, but his lifestyle showed a different course for his life.

3. His mother gave him 200 of the shekels and told her son to use it to make a graven image and a molten image of gods for their worship. Imagine! How's that for a case of stupidity?

4. One day a Levite looking for work came to Micah's home and Micah hired him as his priest.

5. The tribe of Dan was unable to dislodge the Amorites from the coastal land Joshua had assigned them, so they sent scouts to spy out the land. In their travels they came across Micah and his priest in the tribe of Ephraim.

6. When the tribe of Dan moved to the far north to Laish and renamed it Dan, they took Micah's priest, ephod, teraphim, carved and molten images and Levitical priest, who was descended from the line of Moses.

Lesson 13

The Outrageous Act of the Levite to His Concubine and the Punishment of the Benjamites

Judges 19:1–30; 20:1–48; 21:1–25

Judges 21:25 sums up the spiritual state of the pre-monarchic era in Israel: "Everyone did as they saw fit." Therefore, some argue, that this means the following: The Levite in this story represents every Levite; the concubine stands for every woman; the father-in-law represents every host; and the old man in Bethel reminds us of every outsider. The entire narrative is an indication that the world has returned to a Sodom-and-Gomorrah mentality and lifestyle again. Everything in life was in massive chaos, and there were no competent leaders, much less a godly culture, anywhere!

A Levite Retrieves His Concubine Only to Lose Her to Savage Men – 19:1–30

The episode chosen to help us see this awful state of affairs in a sinful nation begins with an unnamed Levite, who lived in the remote area of the hill country of Ephraim, returning home after having traveled south to retrieve his unnamed runaway-concubine from her home and father in Bethlehem of Judah. Whether she had left the Levite four months ago "because she was angry with him" (as in the RSV) or had "played the whore against him" (AV, RV), is debated by scholars; the penalty for adultery was death (Lev. 20:10). However, she is referred to throughout the story as a "young woman" (*han-na῾arah*; 19:3, 4, 5, 6, 8, 9), while 19:1 calls her a "concubine" (*pilegesh*). Verse 2 says "she was 'unfaithful' to him" (*tizneh*, which may also mean she "played the whore," which would fit aspects of "concubine"; or did the text, following the Septuagint, mean to say *tiznach*, "to despise," i.e., she was angry with her husband for some unstated reason?

Is this is to illustrate that Israel had left her husband and Lord God? Israel's relationship was never called a "secondary wife" or "concubine." This would suggest instead that a wife had just gotten tired of playing second fiddle to number-one wife, so she ran back home! But if so, could it be that he could not pay for her keep in those days of a tough economy, so she had to get work by prostitution? Jobs were few, and it wasn't easy to add another person to a household already strapped tight. Selling oneself for sex often was the only employment open to such a woman.

Still, some marital crisis must have arisen between the Levite and his concubine that caused the woman to leave Ephraim and return to Bethlehem. After waiting four months for her to return, the Levite finally decided to go ask her to return home to him. Presumably the second donkey was for her to ride back home on.

The Levite went to the concubine-father's abode, intending to speak to her in a "friendly" way. She probably greeted him as her father appeared at the door. There is an apparent air of happiness, and when this father-in-law saw him, "he rejoiced to meet him." But why was he so happy to see his son-in-law? Because a reconciliation may be in the offing? Or was he needing a male to talk to instead of his daughter's chatter? We don't know.

However, the father-in-law's actions in vv. 4–9 are difficult to sort out. It is clear he wanted the Levite "to remain," "tarry" and "stay for a while" with them in Bethlehem-Judah. When the husband of the concubine got up early to leave for home each day, the father-in-law asked him to stay longer, which he kept doing for four days. Finally, on the fifth day, the Levite was determined to leave (19:8). But the girl's father argued that the day was almost spent, so the two should stay one more night and make their hearts merry (19:9). But the Levite, patience likely used up, left with his concubine.

The Trip Back to Ephraim – 19:10–30

On this fifth time of trying to leave, the Levite had determined to stay no longer and to leave immediately, even though it was late, for he was unwilling to spend another night there (19:10). Off the party of three went for Ephraim (which included the Levite, his servant, and the concubine). As they began their journey, they came near Jerusalem, a mere six miles north of Bethlehem. The servant urged them to stop at Jerusalem for the night, for the day was almost gone (19:11). But the master refused enter a city where the people were not Israelites (19:12); they would press on another six miles to Gibeah or Ramah, which belonged to the tribe of Benjamin.

So, the travelers pressed on to the town of Gibeah, hoping to be given hospitality by one of the Hebrew families there. But that hope would not be fulfilled, for when they arrived, they sat in the city square as the sun rapidly faded—marking the end of that day, just inside the gate of Gibeah. None of the workers returning from the fields took notice or offered them even a place to stay the night. These fellow Israelites were treating them as if they had no relationship to them. The last phrase in v. 15 said it best: "there was no man that took them into his house to lodge." So much for hospitality among the Hebrews! It did not seem to exist at that time!

Later, after sunset, an unidentified old man came in from the fields. As it turned out, he too lived in the hill country of Ephraim. When he saw the travelers, he asked them who they were and where they came from (19:16–17). The Levite explained that they were on their way from Bethlehem in Judah to a remote section of the hill country in Ephraim where they lived—even to the house of the Lord. But not one Benjamite had offered them hospitality, he said (19:18). He added that they had both straw and fodder for the donkeys, and bread and wine for themselves, so they were not longing for a free handout or a meal—neither he nor his male servant nor his maidservant needed anything except lodging for the night (19:19).

The old man graciously responded: "You are welcome [in literal Hebrew, *shalom lak*, "peace to you"] at my house. Let me supply whatever you need. Only don't spend the night in the square" (19:20). He does not say why, but that will become evident in just a while! The state of Israelite society had become so totally rotten from stem to stern that it would be dangerous to remain in the town's square for the night.

After they had gone to the old man's dwelling and were enjoying the food and drink offered them, suddenly they were rudely alerted to the fact that the wicked men of Gibeah had surrounded the house and started pounding loudly on the door, shouting, "Bring out the man who came to your house so we can have sex with him" (19:22). This was a vivid reminder of the profligate manner the men of Sodom had acted in a similar way years ago against Lot when two angels came one night to his house in Sodom (Gen. 19:4–8). Surely this present story was but an echo of the depraved state of affairs that had likewise occurred at Sodom and Gomorrah years ago.

In an effort to dissuade these "worthless men" ('*anshe bene beliyya'al*, "men of the sons of Belial," 19:22), the old man went outside to talk to these renegades. We are uncertain of the meaning of the word "Belial," but *beli* is the negative particle "nothingness, not, without" in combination with *ya'al*, "profit, worth, benefit," so taken together it meant something like "sons of worthlessness" or "men without honor or worth." That they asked for the man who had just arrived in town signals that their desire was homosexual. Such an act was explicitly called an "abomination" in the eyes of God in Leviticus 18:22; 20:13.

The host of the house tried his best to dissuade these men, whom he respectfully addressed as "my brothers," but he also called what they were proposing to do "folly" (*nebalah*, "impiety, wantonness"; the name and meaning of Nabal in 1 Sam. 25:25). And this stranger and his servant, who were in his house, had come under his personal protection per the rules of hospitality in Israel (19:23), so he could not allow what the men demanded.

Amazingly, he offered these vile, brutal men an alternative: They could "humble" the old man's young daughter and the Levite's concubine, and "do with them whatever seemed good to them," but they were not to "do such a vile thing to this man" (19:24). But the men were not pleased even with this crude offer; they had no interest in a woman! He was not identified to them as a Levite, and apparently nor did the servant come into the picture during the debate outside the old farm worker's door.

When the men would not listen, the Levite took his concubine and pushed her out the door like a hunk of meat thrown to dogs—i.e., for the sex-crazed men to savage her, which is exactly what they did. They abused her all night until the morning came (19:25). She returned to the house and collapsed, and in the morning the Levite saw her in the doorway (19:26–27).

One might have thought the 9-1-1 switchboard would have lit up with calls from citizens of Gibeah to come to the rescue, but there was not a word of protest from any Hebrew Benjamite. Righteousness was nowhere to be found in Gibeah! Judgment had to come instead!

The Levite told the woman to get up, but she did not reply. She was lifeless. So, he loaded her on his donkey and set out for home in Ephraim as he had intended (19:27–19:28). Was there no fear of God in that town?

What did this Levite think about on the rest of his trip as he, the donkeys and his servant trotted along toward his place? We do not know, but we know what he did! When he got home, he took a knife and cut up his concubine into twelve parts and sent one part to each of the twelve tribes of Israel (19:29). Now when all Israel saw a piece of the corpse, the everyone said that such an atrocious thing had never been seen "since the day the Israelites came up out of Egypt." This was followed by a public appeal: "Think about her!" (Literally: *simu lakem*, "Set [a response] for yourselves.") The Levite demanded of his fellow citizens: "Speak up!" The nation could no longer just tolerate evil and such unspeakable debauchery as had been done! It was high time for all to repent and to turn back to the Lord. Israel and God needed strong men and women to stand in the gap, for the wall for righteousness had been widely breached!

Nation's Response to a Stonewalled Stance – 20:1–48

At least this event mightily stirred up the nation. They were sufficiently *united* in their outrage that they gathered as a nation at Mizpah[1]—all the Israelites from Dan to Beersheba" (20:1). Three times

---

1. Mizpah may be Tell en-Nasbeh in the hill country of Ephraim about five miles northwest of Gibeah.

they came "with one accord" (20:1, 8, 11). So, something finally had aroused Israel enough to help them see they indeed had drifted far from God. Yes, they had to take action against the tribe of Benjamin for being unwilling to hand over the perpetrators (20:13) of this savage act, even though they spoke of the Benjamites as their "brothers" (20:13, 23, 28).

So Israel turned out at Mizpah with a unified heart and asked either the Levite, the husband of the murdered woman, or the Benjamites: "Tell us how this awful thing happened" (20:3). The Levite related how he and his concubine had stopped at Gibeah in Benjamin for a night's stay. During that night, the house was surrounded by the men of Gibeah, intending to kill him. They took his concubine and raped her until she died. So he took a knife and cut her into pieces and sent part of her to each tribe "because [the men of Gibeah] committed this lewd and this disgraceful act in Israel. Now, all you Israelites, speak up and give your verdict" (20:4–7). The old man who had hosted him, however, was not called on to say anything. The charge stood as the Levite had stated it!

The Israelites' reaction was swift and without dissent. First of all, no one was to return home, for they as a nation were going to attack Gibeah (20:9–10). The tribes sent men throughout the whole tribe of Benjamin, confronting them about this crime and asking the perpetrators be turned over and put to death and purge evil from the land (20:13).

Benjamin was in no mood to concede anything, much less what should be done to the perps; they rallied their men from all the towns of Benjamin to gather in Gibeah to fight their fellow Israelites (20:14–16). Benjamin was able to field 26,000 swordsmen along with 700 crack troops. These 700 were especially equipped as left-handed stone-slingers who were able to hit targets the size of a hair's length (20:16).

The Three Battles Against Benjamin Ensued – 20:18–48

This situation and the battles it raised must have been very important for the writer of Scripture, for he devotes an extraordinary amount of space to what took place. Especially significant must have been the final battle, for it has the largest amount of textual coverage of the three battles.

The First Battle – 20:18–21

The eleven tribes of Israel went up *en masse* to Bethel, where they inquired of Elohim as to who should fight the Benjamites first. (Note they do not use "Jehovah," the covenantal name for God, but just "Elohim.") The tribe of Judah was chosen to go against Benjamin first. This may make some sense, for the murdered concubine was from Bethlehem in Judah.

The men of Judah rose early in the morning and pitched their tents near Gibeah as they initiated their attack on Benjamin, but things were not going to turn out as expected. Even though the Benjamites were vastly outnumbered by the other eleven tribes, the Benjamites slaughtered 22,000 Israelite troops. It was an overwhelming victory for Benjamin; but how could that be when they were the ones being punished? Where was God in this whole mess? There was, even more surprisingly, no mention made of the number of Benjamites who had fallen in battle.

The Second Battle – 20:22–25

The men of Israel tried to encourage each other despite such a horrible loss of life and such a defeat as they once again took up the same positions (20:22). But instead of rushing right into the battle, the Israelite army first went up to the sanctuary to weep before the Lord until evening to see if there was any new word from him, for how could they have clearly understood his word yesterday when 22,000 had fallen in a battle the Lord seemed to approve of? This time they did not ask who should go up next. They asked if they should go up at all against the Benjamites. (20:23). The divine answer was, Yes, "Go up against them." (20:23c).

So for a second time the battle against Benjamin was joined, but the results were almost as startling; another 18,000 Israelite swordsmen from the eleven tribes died (20:24). How could this be happening? They had sought the Lord's direction, and he'd told them to go and fight.

Before the Third Battle – 20:26–48

Things could not have gotten any worse. Now all the people went up to the sanctuary in Bethel and sat there weeping before the Lord (20:26).

A fast was proclaimed to be observed until evening when Israel presented to the Lord burnt and fellowship offerings (20:26b). The Ark of the Covenant was there; the one who ministered at the altar was Phineas the son of Eleazar, the son of Aaron (20:27). Once more Israel asked, "Shall we [all] go up again to battle with Benjamin, our brother, or not?" (20:28).

This time the LORD answered, "Go, for tomorrow I will give them into your hands" (20:28b).

The First Phase of the Third Battle – 20:29–34

In two previous battles, the Israelite army had been thoroughly routed, and they lost 40,000 in total. By now Benjamin must have been feeling invincible, for despite being vastly outnumbered, they'd had two decisive victories. The writer does not pause to clue us readers in on what is being said on the Benjamite side. But Benjamin had little idea what God had in store for them.

The armies took up similar battle stations as they had in the prior confrontations. But key to this battle was the emplacement of an ambush around Gibeah. The battle seemed to be taking the same routine formation as thirty Israelite men fell in the fields. But then Israel's strategy kicked in, which was to lure the Benjamites away from the town. Meanwhile, Israel had hidden troops at Baal Tamar, on the west of Gibeah (20:33). Then 10,000 of Israel's special troops met up with some of the army coming out of Gibeah. The plan seemed to be operating as planned.

The Second Phase of the Third Battle – 20:35–41

The Benjamites began to sense how the battle was shaping up, for the Israelite troops had fallen back and lured them a good ways away from Gibeah. Also, the Lord was defeating the Benjamites, for he struck down 25,100 men from that tribe. The verb used in v. 35 is from the root *nagaph*, "to strike, to hit," the same verb used in the plagues of Egypt. With the Lord now in the battle, one could expect the results to change dramatically.

Now that the troops had been drawn out of Gibeah, it was time for the Israelite ambush to rush into Gibeah, put the whole city to the sword and set it on fire (20:37). When the Israelite retreating troops saw the smoke rising from the city, they turned around and pressed the Benjamites head-on. At that time, seeing a "great cloud of smoke" rising from their hometown, became terrified (20:40–41). This time, the Benjamites realized, the battle was not going to be like it had been previously.

The Third Phase of the Third Battle – 20:42–48

Now that the inhabitants of Gibeah had seen that their village was being consumed with fire and that the Israelites had turned from fleeing from them to now face them, they were terrified (20:41). There was only one thing to do: They had to flee from the *Israelites* in the direction of the desert; but they could not escape the ravages of the battle (20:42), for now the Israelites who had set the town of Gibeah on fire came to cut them down as they were trapped between the two lines of attack (20:42b). The two groups of Israelite fighters surrounded the men of Benjamin and easily overran them so that 18,000 Benjamites fell dead on the east side of Gibeah (20:43).

As the Benjamites fled toward the desert to the rock of Rimmon (meaning "pomegranate"), Israel cut down another 5000 men along the roads. Israel maintained a heavy pressure on the Benjamites all the way to Gidom, where another 2000 were cut down as they fled. The Rimmon rock, where some 600 fugitives turned for refuge, may have been the el-Jaia Cave in the Wadi es-Swenit, a little over a mile from Gibeah. Here there was a 30-meter-high-cave, with hundreds of smaller caves and pits inside, resembling a split pomegranate.[2] The remaining men of Benjamin stayed there away from their city of Gibeah for four months.

Meanwhile, the men of Israel went back to the tribe of Benjamin and put the rest of the towns of that tribe to the sword, including all humans and animals in a *herem-like* fashion. It seemed Benjamin was removed as a tribe, having been totally wiped out as a people (20:46–48). The impact of this fact must have hit Israel hard!

---

2. Daniel I. Block, *The New American Commentary, Judges, Ruth*, vol. 6 (1999), 567.

Trying to Figure Out What to Do in Light of Hacking Up the Tribe of Benjamin in Israel – 21:1–24

When Israel had met earlier at Mizpah, they had as a nation vowed to the Lord not to give any of their daughters in marriage to the 600 Benjamites who had escaped to the rock Rimmon (21:1). That decision, however, now raised a serious question as the nation returned to Bethel and sat before "God" [notice: they sat before *Elohim*] until evening. The next day they cried out: "O LORD, why has this happened to Israel? Why should one tribe be missing from Israel today?" (21:3) Was their weeping and crying out just a bunch of crocodile tears and feigned spirituality? Otherwise, how can we explain why they used the name "Elohim," just as they had also opened the solemn assembly in Bethel? We are unsure what the motivation of the people was at this point, but one fact could not be denied: They had just "wiped out" and "cut up" one of the twelve tribes of Israel from existing among them. When Israel came to the realization that one tribe had been "cut off" or "hacked off" from Israel, they used a verb that appears only here in the Old Testament, though it uses the same root as is found in the name of Gideon. The word is *gada`*, "hacker." They also used the passive form of this verb "to hack," leaving it an unsolved question as to who was really responsible for this excision of the tribe of Benjamin from the nation of Israel.

The people decided the next day to build an altar and to offer up on it burnt offerings and fellowship offerings to the Lord (21:4). But what was his intention through all this commotion and dying? Did God still care if Benjamin was able to still exist after this? Was he thinking ahead of future leaders who would come from this tribe later in history like the Apostle Paul and the line of David? If so, how would the Lord have solved the fact that the tribes had all sworn a vow that none would give any daughters as wives to the 600 remaining Benjamite men? There was no word from God at this juncture; Israel seemed to solve the issue by plans designed among themselves! The nation was deeply troubled and sorrowed over the fact that one whole tribe had just been severed (21:6).

The way Israel responded to this crisis was to ask who among the people in the nation had not showed up to fight against Benjamin and thus had not taken the solemn vow to deny any daughters to any the remaining Benjamite men (21:5). Quickly the answer came, for when they counted the people, they learned that the men from Jabesh Gilead (meaning "well-drained soil of Gilead") had not shown up (21:8–9). That suggested a possible solution! Jabesh Gilead was located somewhere along the modern wadi of el-Yabis, an east west tributary of the Jordan River that cuts across Gilead, perhaps at a site seven miles east of the Jordan.

The nation adopted the following plan of providing women for the 600 men at the rock Rimmon by sending 12,000 fighting men to attack Jabesh Gilead and put every living thing to death except any woman who was a virgin (21:10–11). The fighting detachment was able to carry out this order by using the law of *herem*, or the "ban" (Num. 21:2–3). But even this involved some casuistic thinking and acting, for that law required sparing none of that population, but dedicating everyone and everything to destruction, or to the Lord. However, in the earlier case of the Israelites who sinned by worshiping Baal-Peor in the days of Moses (Num. 25:1–18), the troops returned with children and women, but they were to preserve the women who had never known a man (Num. 31:13–20), so that would be the way Israel may have provided the precedent for Jabesh-Gilead to act. By this method the troops discovered 400 virgin women.

Scripture doesn't say how they distinguished the virgins from those who weren't. One rabbi offered this idea: He would have every female child stand before the High Priest to be cross-examined. All whose faces turned pale when questioned if they had slept with a man were one category of women, for they would express it so by the fact that their faces would blush with fire.[3] Whatever the method, it yielded 400 women, who were then brough across the Jordan "to the [Israelite] camp at Shiloh in Canaan "(21:12b). But that was a surprise, for why had they not been brought to Bethel or Mizpah? Why Shiloh? Some say they did that for psychological reasons: to overcome the possible reluctance of the surviving Benjamites to go to those holy sites, whereas Shiloh was a neural place. Perhaps!

Since this method left them 200 women short of supplying wives for all 600 Benjamite men, the people of Israel still mourned over the eradication of one whole tribe in the land (21:15). Then a new idea struck them (*hinneh*, "behold"), for there in Israel was an annual festival of the Lord in Shiloh. So, they instructed the 200 wifeless Benjamites to hide in the vineyards and watch for the time when the girls' dance would occur. Then, at the opportune moment, the 200 men were to rush out and choose a girl for a wife (21:19–21). If the fathers or brothers of these captured girls complained, the elders added, they would ask them to do them the "kindness" of helping them to solve this problem. Anyway, none would be guilty of breaking the vow, for they had not given their daughters; the men had chosen them (21:22b).

The identity of this "annual festival of the LORD" is not given. The three festivals traditionally are the Feast of Passover and Unleavened Bread, the Feast of Weeks, Harvest, or Pentecost, and the Feast of Firstfruits (Exod. 23:16; 34:22; Num. 28:26). None of these are mentioned.

The Benjamites acted as instructed; thus, while the girls danced, each man ran out and caught one girl and carried her off to be his wife (21:23). These men returned to the devastated towns of Benjamin and rebuilt the towns and settled in them (21:23b). With that accomplished, the families of Israel returned to their homes, each to his own inheritance (21:24).

---

3. J. Milgrom, *Numbers*, JPS Torah Commentary (1990), 259, cited in Block, 575.

Conclusions

1. A concubine belonging to a Levite living in Ephraim ran away to the south, back to her father's home in Bethlehem of Judah. After four months of absence the Levite went to retrieve her. Her father, however, kept delaying the couple's leaving and their return home for four days.

2. Late on the fifth day, the Levite, his servant, his concubine and two donkeys headed north, deliberately passing Jerusalem as a place to stay until they came to the town of Gibeah of the Benjamites. The men of Benjamin returning from their work in the fields all selfishly passed their fellow Israelites up, with no one offering any hospitality until one old man came back from the fields and offered them lodging for the night in his place in Gibeah.

3. The men of Gibeah that night banged on the old man's door, demanding the man who had just come to their town. The old-timer refused to break the rules for hosting a male guest, so he amazingly offered his daughter and the Levites's concubine instead, whom the Benjamites abused all night so that by morning she was found dead on the old man's doorstep.

4. The Levite cut up the corpse of his concubine into twelve pieces and sent one part to each tribe in Israel. Shocked, Israel came together at Mizpah and asked Benjamin to hand over the perps to be punished. When they refused, the nation fought Benjamin until there were only 600 men remaining alive in that whole tribe of Benjamin.

5. The 600 Benjamites fled to Rimmon Rock, where Israel spoke to them peaceably to meet them at Shiloh where they would give them, at first, 400 virgin girls as wives, taken from the destruction of Jabesh Gilead for that city's failure to come up to fight the battle just completed.

6. The remaining 200 girls were gotten by the men who were still without wives from the girls involved in a sort of Sadie-Hawkins dance at an annual festival in Shiloh wherein each rushed out and claimed a wife!

⊡ Messianic Jewish
Publishers & Resources

*We are a
three-fold ministry,
reaching Jewish people
with the message of Messiah,
teaching our non-Jewish
spiritual family about
their Jewish roots,
and strengthening
congregations with
excellent resources.*

Over 100 Messianic Jewish
Books, Bibles &
Commentaries available at
your favorite Bookstore.

Endorsed by
Christian Leaders
and Theologians:

Dr. Jack Hayford
Dr. Walter C. Kaiser, Jr.
Dr. Marvin Wilson
Ken Taylor
Stephen Strang
Dr. R.C. Sproul
Coach Bill McCartney
and more!

800-410-7367
www.MessianicJewish.net

Printed in the United States
by Baker & Taylor Publisher Services